The
Politics
of
Social Ecology

The Politics

of

Social Ecology

$\blacksquare\!=\!=\!=\!\blacksquare$

Libertarian Municipalism

Janet Biehl

with

Murray Bookchin

BLACK
ROSE
BOOKS

Montreal ✖ *New York* ✖ *London*

Black Rose Books No.AA259
ISBN: 1-55164-100-3 (bound)
ISBN: 1-55164-101-1 (pbk.)
Library of Congress Catalog Card Number: 97-074155

Canadian Cataloguing in Publication Data

Biehl, Janet, 1953-

    The politics of social ecology : libertarian municipalism

ISBN: 1-55164-100-3 (bound)
ISBN: 1-55164-101-1 (pbk.)

1. Municipal government. 2. Social ecology.
3. Libertarianism. I Bookchin, Murray, 1921- II. Title.

HT151.B665 1998   320.8   C97-900726-7

C.P. 1258   250 Sonwil Drive   99 Wallis Road
Succ. Place du Parc   Buffalo, New York   London, E9 5LN
Montréal, Québec   14225 USA   England
H2W 2R3
Canada
To order books in North America: (phone) 1-800-565-9523
(fax) 1-800-221-9985
In Europe: (phone) 081-986-485 (fax) 081-533-5821

Our Web site address: http://web.net/blackrosebooks

Printed in Canada

Table of Contents

Author's Note

Libertarian municipalism, the political dimension of the broader body of ideas known as social ecology, was developed over the course of several decades by the anarchist social theorist Murray Bookchin. It is the culmination of a lifetime of his thinking about how society might best be radically transformed in a humane and rational way.

Part of the international Communist left since his youth in the 1930s, Bookchin has devoted his life to looking for ways to replace today's capitalist society, which immiserates most of humanity and poisons the natural world, with a more enlightened and rational alternative. A close student of the European revolutionary tradition, he is best known for introducing the idea of ecology into leftist thought, and for first positing in 1962 that a liberatory society would also have to be an ecological society.

For most of this century, the existence of the Soviet Union created massive problems for the left, especially since it appeared to wed a century of revolutionary aspirations for a good society with a barbaric system of totalitarianism, gulags and mass executions. The blow inflicted by this misalliance is one from which the left is still reeling. No less than his fellow leftists, Bookchin has had to grapple with the problem of rescuing this tradition from its Stalinist desecration.

Bookchin himself had departed from the Communist movement as a young man in the mid-1930s and had been a critic of vulgar Marxism thereafter: for its authoritarianism, for its instrumentalism, for its absence of ethics. But his personal departure from the Communist movement was not an abandonment of the revolutionary project; on the contrary, he proceeded to recast it in libertarian terms, drawing upon the best of the anarchist and Marxist traditions to create a unique synthesis that he called social ecology. The society he foresaw would be one that eliminated not only capitalism but the Nation-State, not only classes but hierarchies, not only exploitation but domination and that constituted a rational and ecological alternative.

If Bookchin drew a critique of capitalism from Marxism, he has drawn ideas of communalism, anti-Statism, and confederalism from the anarchist tradition. Yet anarchism, too, has not been immune to his criticism. In contrast to many anarchists of an individualistic bent, Bookchin is no enemy of institutions as such. Freedom that is conceived entirely in personal terms, that has no institutional embodiment, he argues, languishes as a narcissistic indulgence. A society that sustains both individual and social freedom, must be undergirded by institutions that are themselves liberatory. It must provide the structural means by which citizens can collectively manage their own affairs. The question, then, is not whether a free society will have institutions, but what kind.

A crucial part of Bookchin's project has been to identify the revolutionary "forms of freedom" that give organizational substance to the idea of freedom. After decades of historical study and political engagement, he began writing about libertarian municipalism in 1972.

In brief, libertarian municipalism seeks to revive the democratic possibilities latent in existing local governments and transform them into direct democracies. It aims to decentralize these political communities so that they are humanly scaled and tailored to their natural environments. It aims to restore the practices and qualities of citizenship, so that men and women can collectively take responsibility for managing their own communities, according to an ethics of sharing and cooperation, rather than depend on elites. Once direct democracies have been created, the democratized municipalities could be knit together into confederations that could ultimately present a challenge to capitalism and the Nation-State, leading to a rational ecological anarchist society.

By the late 1970s and early 1980s, when he had fully developed these ideas, they influenced a variety of grassroots movements in the United States and Europe. Today, they potentially have even greater significance, for the collapse of the

Soviet Union–despite its desecration of the revolutionary tradition–has paradoxically produced disarray on the left and neces-
sitated a search for a new direction, a new way to empower people in a liberatory society.

Nor is it only the current leftist dilemma for which
Bookchin's ideas have relevance. Across the American political
spectrum, a wide variety of thinkers are lamenting the eviscera-
tion of the civic sphere in the United States today. Not only the
left but the center and even the right are all bewailing the decline
of community life and civic participation. On this issue too
Bookchin's municipal approach offers a radical-left perspective.

Finally, around the world, transnational capital is creating a giant market in which incalculable profits are reaped by the
few, plunging the many into poverty and despair, obliterating traditional societies, and poisoning the biosphere. Bookchin's libertarian municipalism explores the institutions that could potentially arrest this rapacious system of exploitation and biocide.

To date, unfortunately, Bookchin's published writings on
libertarian municipalism have not received the wide public attention that they deserve. One reason for this may be that they are
not as accessible as they might be. Many of his articles appear in
hard-to-find periodicals, while his own book *From Urbanization
to Cities*, rich as it is in historical and theoretical material, is massive enough in scope and execution to be formidable to many
readers.

For some years it has seemed to me that a concise and
abbreviated exposition was needed that would make the ideas of
libertarian municipalism more accessible to the general reader.
Hence this book, which is intended as a brief, introductory
overview. I have made no attempt to interpret, analyze, or assess
libertarian municipalism. Rather, my purpose has been to provide a straightforward synopsis of its basic points as Bookchin
developed them, including a sketch of the historical context in
which he set them. I have also attempted to provide material on
the practical aspects of organizing a libertarian municipalist
movement. Let me emphasize that the ideas that appear in these
pages are all Bookchin's; only their articulation is mine. In the
interview that appears in the second part of the book, I have

raised with Bookchin some of the questions that in my ten-year association with him, I have heard most frequently asked in discussions of these ideas.

I am grateful to Bookchin for his support for this project and for the interview. Let me emphasize that the ideas that appear in these pages are all Bookchin's; only their articulation is mine. In the interview that appears in the second part of the book, I have raised with Bookchin some of the questions that in my ten-year association with him, I have heard most frequently asked in discussions of these ideas. He read the manuscript in draft and commented on it, to its immense benefit. Cindy Milstein and Gary Sisco also read an early draft and made invaluable suggestions, for which they have my warm thanks. Dimitri Roussopoulos of Black Rose Books has my deep gratitude for his unflagging support for this project.

I have tried to present these ideas in the simplest possible terms, for the benefit of readers who are wholly unfamiliar with them. Bookchin's own writings contain philosophical and historical nuances that are absent here. Readers who are interested in learning more about libertarian municipalism and should of course consult the writings listed at the end of this book. In no way should this book be considered a substitute for Bookchin's original works, only a summary introduction to them.

It is my hope that libertarian municipalism will become a touchstone for the resuscitation of the left, in a time of its weakness and disarray. I believe that these ideas could be fruitful for the left on an international scale. Probably inevitably, my presentation is refracted through the prism of the culture in which I live and write; I hope that readers outside the United States will be able to interpret the main principles in the context of their own cultures.

Janet Biehl
Burlington, Vermont
November 27, 1996

Chapter 1

Politics versus Statecraft

Libertarian municipalism is one of many political theories that concern themselves with the principles and practices of democracy. In contrast to most such theories, however, it does not accept the conventional notion that the State and governmental systems typical of Western countries today are truly democracies. On the contrary, it considers them republican States with pretensions of being democratic. Republican States, to be sure, are more "democratic" than other kinds of States, like monarchies and dictatorships, in that they contain various kinds of representative institutions.

But they are nonetheless States—overarching structures of domination in which a few people rule over the great majority. A State, by its very nature, is structurally and professionally separated from the general population—in fact, it is set over and above ordinary men and women. It exercises power over them, making decisions that affect their lives. Its power in the last instance rests on violence, over whose legal use the State has a monopoly, in the form of its armies and police forces. In a structure where power is distributed so unevenly, democracy is impossible. Far from embodying rule by the people, even a republican State is incompatible with popular rule.

Libertarian municipalism advances a kind of democracy, by contrast, that is no mere fig leaf for State rule. The democracy it advances is direct democracy—in which citizens in communities manage their own affairs through face-to-face processes of deliberation and decision-making, rather than have the State do it for them.

In contrast to theories of representative "democracy," libertarian municipalism makes a sharp distinction between politics and Statecraft. In conventional use, to be sure, these concepts are nearly synonymous. Politics, as we normally think of it, is an essential component of representative systems of government. It is the set of procedures and practices by which "the people" choose a small group of individuals—politicians—to speak for them and represent them in a legislative or executive body.

These politicians, in politics-as-we-know-it, are affiliated with political parties, which are supposed to be associations of people who share a commitment to a particular political agenda or philosophy; the politicians who belong to a party, in theory, speak for its agenda and advance its philosophy. As an election for governmental office approaches, various parties put forth politicians as candidates and, assisted by many consultants, wage electoral campaigns to try to persuade citizens to vote for them. Each party touts its own candidate's suitability for office and disparages that of its rivals. During the campaign the candidates express their respective positions on the important issues of the day, which clarifies their differences, in order that voters may grasp the full range of choices that they have.

Hopefully, after carefully weighing the issues and soberly judging the positions of each candidate, the voters—who have now become an "electorate"—make their choice. The contenders whose positions accord most fully with those of the majority are rewarded by being granted the office they covet. Upon entering the corridors of government, such is the belief, these new officeholders will labour tirelessly on behalf of those who voted for them (who by now have gained yet another appellation, "constituents"). Scrupulously they adhere to the commitments they avowed during their electoral campaigns, or so we are told. Indeed, as they cast their votes on legislation or otherwise make decisions, their primary loyalty is allegedly to the positions supported by their "constituents." As a result, when a piece of legislation or an executive order or any other type of action is taken, it reflects the will of the majority of citizens.

It should be clear to any sensate reader that this sketch is a civics class illusion, and that its "democratic" nature is chimerical. Far from embodying the will of the people, politicians are actually professionals, whose career interests lie in obtaining power precisely through being elected or appointed to higher office. Their electoral campaigns, which only partly or even trivially reflect the concerns of ordinary men and women, more often use the mass media to sway and manipulate their concerns, or even generate spurious concerns as distractions. The manipulative nature of this system has been particularly egregious in recent U.S. elections, where, financed by big money, political campaigns focus increasingly on trivial but emotionally volatile issues, diverting the attention of the "electorate" and masking the deep-seated problems that have real effects on their lives. The programs the candidates run on are ever more vacuous, loaded with ever more pabulum—and by general acknowledgment, have less and less connection to the candidate's future behaviour in office.

Once they have gained office, indeed, politicians quite commonly renege on their avowed campaign commitments. Instead of attending to the needs of those who cast their ballots for them or advancing the policies they supported, they usually find it more rewarding to serve the monied interest groups that are eager to enhance their careers. Vast sums of money are required in order to wage an electoral campaign in the first place, and candidates are therefore dependent upon big donors to get themselves into office. To one degree or another, then, those who are elected to represent the people are likely to end up advancing policies that protect the interests of established wealth rather than those of the group they supposedly represent.

Politicians make such choices not because they are "bad people"—indeed, many of them originally enter public service with idealistic motivations. Rather, they make these choices because they have become part of a system of power interactions whose imperatives have come to rule over them. This system of power interactions, let it be said candidly, is the State itself, dominated by big money. By functioning in the framework of this system, they come to share its aims of securing and maintaining a monopoly of power for an elite group of professionals, and of protecting and advancing the interests of the wealthy, rather than the more popular aims of empowering the many and redistributing wealth.

The political parties with which "politicians" are associated, in turn, are not necessarily groups of high-minded citizens who share like political views. They are essentially hierarchically structured, top-down bureaucracies that are seeking to gain State power for themselves through their candidates. Their main concerns are the practical exigencies of faction, power, and mobilization, not the social well-being of the officeholders' "constituents," except insofar as professions of concern for the well-being of ordinary men and women attracts votes. But in no sense are these kinds of political parties either derivative of the body politic or constituted by it. Far from expressing the will of citizens, parties function precisely to contain the body politic, to control it and to manipulate it—indeed, to prevent it from developing an independent will.

However much political parties may be in competition with each other and however much they may genuinely disagree on some specific issues, all of them share in assenting to the existence of the State and operating within its magisterial parameters. Every party that is out of power is in effect a "shadow" State waiting to take power—a State-in-waiting.

To label this system politics is a gross misnomer; it should more properly be called Statecraft. Professionalized, manipulative, and immoral, these systems of elites and masses impersonate democracy, making a mockery of the democratic ideals to which they cynically swear fealty in periodic appeals to the "electorate." Far from empowering people as citizens, Statecraft presupposes the general abdication of citizen power. It reduces citizens to "taxpayers" and "voters" and "constituents," as if they were too juvenile or too incompetent to manage public affairs themselves. They are expected to function merely passively and let elites look out for their best interests. They are to participate in "politics" mainly on election days, when "voter turnout" gives legitimacy to the system itself—and on tax days, of course, when they finance it. The rest of the year, the masters of Statecraft would prefer that people tend to their private affairs and disregard the activities of "politicians." Indeed, insofar as people slough off their passivity and begin to take an active interest in political life, they may create problems for the State by calling attention to the discrepancies between social reality and the rhetoric that it espouses.

Politics as Direct Democracy

Despite their interchangeability in conventional usage, politics is not at all the same thing as Statecraft; nor is the State its natural domain. In past centuries, before the emergence of the Nation-State, politics was understood to mean the activity of citizens in a public body, empowered in shared, indeed participatory institutions. In contrast to the State, politics, as it once was and as it could be again, is directly democratic. As advanced by libertarian municipalism, it is the direct management of community affairs by citizens through face-to-face democratic institutions, especially popular assemblies.

In today's mass society the prospect that people could manage their own affairs in such assemblies may seem woefully remote. Yet the times in history when people did so are nearer to us than we may think. Direct democracy was essential to the political tradition that Western societies claim to cherish— it lies at its very fountainhead. For the democratic political tradition originated not with the Nation-State but with the face-to-face democracy of ancient Athens, in the middle of the fifth century B.C.E. Politics, as it was first described in the writings of Aristotle, originally denoted a direct democracy—the very word *politics* is etymologically derived from *polis*, the ancient Greek word (commonly mistranslated as "city-state") for the public, participatory dimension of a community.

In the Athenian polis, direct democracy attained a remarkable degree of realization. During one of the most astonishing periods in European, indeed world history—between the eighth and fifth centuries B.C.E.—Athenian men and their spokesmen, like Solon, Cleisthenes, and Pericles (all three, ironically, renegade aristocrats), gradually dismembered the traditional feudal system that had been endemic to Homeric times and created institutions that opened public life to every adult Athenian male. Power ceased to be the prerogative of a small, aristocratic stratum and became instead a citizen activity. At high water the body politic of ancient Athens probably consisted of some forty thousand adult male citizens. (Unfortunately, it excluded women, slaves, and resident aliens, including Aristotle himself, from political participation.)

The ancient Athenians had a strikingly different concept of political life from the one to which most people in today's Western "democracies" are accustomed. Today we most often regard individuals as essentially private beings who sometimes find it necessary or expedient to enter public life, perhaps against their will, in order to protect or advance their private concerns. In the common present-day view, political participation is a (usually) unpleasant but nonetheless unavoidable extraneous burden that must be borne stoically before one returns to one's "real life" in the private sphere.

By contrast, the ancient Athenians thought that adult Greek men are inherently political beings, that it is in their nature to consociate with one another in order to organize and manage their shared community life. Although their nature has both political and private components, the Athenians believed, their distinctive humanity lies in the political component. As political beings, then, Greek men cannot be fully human unless they participate in organized community life; without their participation there is no community life, indeed no organized community—and no freedom.

Unlike the professionals who run the citadels of State power today and perform the machinations of Statecraft, the ancient Athenians maintained a system of self-governance that was consciously amateur in character. Its institutions—especially its almost-weekly meetings of the citizens' assembly and its judicial system structured around huge juries—made it possible for political participation to be broad, general, and ongoing. Most civic officials were selected from among the citizens by lot and were frequently rotated. It was a community in which citizens had the competence not only to govern themselves but to assume office when chance summoned them to do so.

The direct democracy of Athens waned in the aftermath of the Peloponnesian war, and during the Roman Empire and afterward the idea of democracy itself received a bad name as congruent with "mob rule," especially from political theorists and writers who served imperial, kingly, or ecclesiastical masters. But the notion of politics as popular self-management was never wholly extinguished; to the contrary, both the idea and its reality have persisted in the centuries that span those eras and ours. In the town centres of many medieval European communes, in colonial New England, and in revolutionary Paris, among many other places, citizens congregated to discuss and manage the community in which they lived. Popes, princes, and kings, to be sure, often developed overarching structures of power, but at the local level, in villages, towns, and neighbourhoods, people controlled much of their own community life well into modern times.

It must be conceded at the outset that history affords us no example of an ideal direct democracy. All of the notable instances of it, including ancient Athens, were greatly flawed by patriarchal and other oppressive features. Nevertheless, the best features of these instances can be culled and assembled to form a composite political realm that is neither parliamentary nor bureaucratic, neither centralized nor professionalized, but democratic and political.

Here at the base of society rich political cultures flourished. Daily public discussions bubbled up in squares and parks, on street corners, in schools, cafés, and clubs, wherever people gathered informally. Many of the neighbourhood plazas in ancient, medieval, and Renaissance cities were places where citizens spontaneously congregated, argued out their problems, and decided on courses of action. These lively political cultures encompassed cultural aspects as well as explicitly political ones, with civic rituals, festivals, celebrations, and shared expressions of joy and mourning. In villages, towns, neighbourhoods, and cities political participation was a self-formative process, in which citizens, by virtue of their ability to manage their community's pursuits, developed not only a rich sense of cohesion as a political body but a rich individual selfhood.

The Recreation of Politics

With the rise and consolidation of Nation-States, centralized power began to stifle this public participation, subjecting even distant localities to State control and terminating whatever autonomy they had hitherto enjoyed. At first this invasion was carried out in the name of monarchs claiming a divinely sanctioned privilege to rule, but even after the concept of democracy became an object of passionate popular aspiration in the early nineteenth century, builders of republican States appropriated it as a gloss for their "representative" institutions—parliaments and congresses—and at the same time as a mantle to cloak their elitist, paternalistic, and coercive nature. So it is that Western Nation-States today are routinely referred to as "democracies" without a murmur of objection. With the creation of the welfare or Social State, the State's powers—as well as its acceptability to the unwary—were even further expanded, assuming many of the social tasks for which communities had once been responsible on their own account.

Still, in most parts of the European and American world, political life remained to some degree alive at the local level, as it does to this day. Direct democracy, of course, no longer exists in the ancient Athenian sense. Yet even in communities that have been stripped of their former proud powers, formal and informal political arenas still abide—civic associations, town meetings, forums, issue-oriented initiatives, and the like—as venues for face-to-face public processes. That is, even if direct democracy no longer exists, local public spheres do persist.

To be sure, those remnant public spheres are themselves being gravely undermined today, as larger social forces corrode neighbourhood and community life. Economic pressures are forcing people to spend ever more of their time earning a livelihood, which leaves them with less time to devote even to socializing or to family life, let alone to community affairs. The ethos of consumption in capitalist society draws men and women to give over much of what free time that they do have to shopping, even as a form of recreation, or else to television-watching, which primes them for more shopping. As family life becomes by necessity a "haven in a heartless world," political life comes to recede ever further from their grasp. In such a situation neither political life nor family life can flourish.

Thus, the very meaning of politics is gradually being forgotten. People in Western societies are losing their memory of politics as an active, vital process of self-management, while the enervated concept of citizenship—as voting and tax-paying and the passive receipt of State-provided services—is mistaken for citizenship itself. Deracinated from community, the individual is isolated and powerless, alone in a mass society that has little use for him or her as a political being.

But if people lack apparent interest in public life, as so many commentators today lament, it may be because public life lacks meaning—that is, because it lacks substantial power. Instead of residing in local political realms, most decision-making power lies in the hands of the State. It did not get there by accident, or an act of God, or a force of nature. It was placed there by human agency. Builders of States appropriated it, compelling or seducing people to surrender their power to the larger edifice.

But power, having been taken from the people, can also be recovered by them once again. It should come as no surprise that in all parts of the Euro-American world today men and women are increasingly rejecting the existing party system and the paltry political role that has been doled out to them by the State. Alienation from what passes for "political" processes has become widespread—witness massive voting abstentions—while "politicians" are distrusted far and wide. Even when pandered to extravagantly, citizens increasingly react with disgust and even hostility to electoral manipulation. Such revulsion against the processes of Statecraft is a salutary trend, one on which a libertarian municipalist politics can build.

The project of libertarian municipalism is to resuscitate politics in the older sense of the word—to construct and expand local direct democracy, such that ordinary citizens make decisions for their communities and for their society as a whole. It is not, it should be understood, an attempt to expand citizen involvement in the processes of the republican State. It is not a call for greater voter turnout at the next election, or for citizen mobilization in influencing legislation ("write your representative"), or even for expanding the use of tools like the initiative, referendum, and recall with the intention of "democratizing" the Nation-State. Nor is it an attempt to replace winner-take-all voting systems (typical of the United States, Britain, and Canada) with proportional representation, to allow members of small or third parties to gain office in accordance with the votes they receive. In short, it does not seek to embroider upon the "democratic" veils of the State, by working for "democratic reforms." Least of all does it encourage men and women to actively participate in a structure that, all its masquerades to the contrary, is geared to control them. Libertarian municipalism, in fact, is antithetical to the State since the State as such is unassimilable with community self-management and a thriving civic sphere.

It is the aim of libertarian municipalism, rather, to revive the public sphere that is being precipitately lost, and to transform it into a political realm. It is to engender active citizens out of passive constituents and endow them with a political context in which they have meaningful choices. It aims to create this context by institutionalizing their power in neighbourhood assemblies and town meetings. In a very radical sense, libertarian municipalism goes back to the very roots of politics, to revive direct democracy and expand it, along with the rational and ethical virtues and practices that support it.

Chapter 2

The Historical City

Before we discuss the specific libertarian municipalist project of reviving the political realm, we must spend a few chapters examining the nature of that realm, to clarify just what we mean when we refer to it. The political realm, it should be understood, has a social context, even an anthropological and historical context, as well as specific traditions that have developed over the centuries.

Perhaps most crucially, the political realm must be understood as one of three realms that are endemic to human societies generally: the political realm, the social realm, and the State.*

The Social Realm

The social realm (not to be confused with society as a whole) is the private realm, encompassing production and economic life. More anciently, it is also the personal arena of family life, of care and friendship, of self-maintenance and reproduction, and of consangineal obligation. The existence of family groups as such is constant across human cultures; despite the disparate forms that societies take, it is in family groups that individuals fraternize in the greatest degree of intimacy. The social realm may thus be demarcated as a cross-cultural phenomenon, inherent in human communities.

The social realm is by far the oldest of the three realms. From their earliest emergence in prehistory as bands and tribes, human communities were structured around the social realm; indeed, it constituted the largest part of those societies. At the band or tribe's core the social realm was rooted in the domestic world of women. It was complemented by a nascent civil world inhabited by men, but since this civil realm was very limited and the State did not yet exist at all, group life in the earliest societies was virtually coeval with the social realm.

In keeping with their familistic nature, band and tribal societies were organized according to the ostensibly "natural" biological principle of kinship. The blood tie, the principle of consanguinity, was the shared bond that held a tribe together; all members of a given tribe were said to be related by blood, to be descended from a common ancestor—that common descent was what made them all members of the same tribe. The blood tie did not have to be literal; when necessary, a tribe could willfully expand it beyond actual kinship to the point of fiction— for example, when strangers were coopted into the tribe, or in the case of intertribal marriages. Such alliances were legitimated by virtue of being pronounced in kinship terms. Still, even if it often had to be stretched, kinship was the customary principle that defined and ideologically undergirded a unitary tribe.

Nor was kinship the only "natural" biological principle around which tribal society was organized. The biological fact of sex marked the various responsibilities of tribal life as either male or female, producing gendered divisions of labour and even of culture. The biological fact of age became still another touchstone for social organization: members who had lived longer, especially in preliterate societies, were honoured as the repositories of a tribe's customs and wisdom, a status that allowed some older members even to claim supernatural powers, as shamans. All of these "natural" principles had large fictional components and were often honoured in the breach; yet since they were rooted in what seemed to be inalterable bio-

---

*Bookchin makes this tripartite distinction in contrast to many other social theorists who posit only a duality. For example, Aristotle thought in terms of the social and political realms, but not the State (since Athens had none). Hannah Arendt, in *The Human Condition* and other works, essentially followed Aristotle in discussing the social and political realm—but what she called the political realm is actually the State, a misidentification that has generated a certain amount of confusion.

logical facts, they bound these communities together.

In the earliest communities, these biologistic divisions most likely were not rationales for status and rank, let alone for domination and submission. But subsequently male culture came to be considered not only different from women's but of greater value and therefore entitled to dominate it. The elderly's knowledge of tribal wisdom became a warrant for gerontocracy, while kinship became a rationale for belief in the superiority of one tribe over another, giving rise to ethnic chauvinism and racism.

Indeed, an antipathetic relationship between different tribes must have been rooted in tribal society nearly from the outset. Tribes often claimed for themselves the label "the people," in contrast to members of other tribes, whom they essentially regarded as of a different taxonomical order, essentially as nonhuman. This self-identification of a tribe as an effectively distinct species generated a strong ethos of solidarity among its own members—but very often it also gave rise to a vigorous hostility toward members other tribes, who putatively constituted a threat.

Thus bands and tribes dealt warily and often hostilely with outsiders. They might consider strangers who intruded on them to be their deceased ancestors and propitiate them accordingly; or they might regard them as spirit beings, or as spirits of the dead, or as malevolent beings who bore ill intentions toward the tribe—and eliminate them accordingly. To be sure, a tribe might also treat a stranger with hospitality, but that benign attitude usually depended upon the tribe's goodwill in a particular case, or upon its traditional canons of behaviour—or upon its need to build support networks through marriage alliances and to gain adult males to act as its warriors.

The Rise of the City

As their primary means of subsistence, band and tribal societies generally foraged—that is, they hunted animals and gathered vegetation to gain the food, clothing, and shelter that supported their existence; sometimes they engaged in the more transient, swidden forms of horticulture, burning forests to create temporary planting areas for garden crops until the fertility of the soil was exhausted. But at the beginning of the Neolithic period, probably in the Middle East between 10,000 and 7000 B.C.E., a momentous change occurred: Tribal societies gradually shifted their basic means of subsistence away from food gathering and swidden gardening and toward the cultivation of cereal crops. That is, instead of moving around to obtain food from relatively transient sources, tribespeople settled down into stable, even permanent villages and systematically cultivated grains and domesticated animals.

This transition to Neolithic culture—to farming and animal husbandry—spread quickly and widely throughout Eurasia and had repercussions in many aspects of social life, transforming tribal society into a new dispensation altogether. Grain being less perishable than meat and vegetation, supplies of food could now be held in reserve, in storage, which made it possible for some members of the tribe to control the distribution of the food supply. A fraction of the members thus became owners of property and ultimately of wealth, giving rise to class formations. Classes, in turn, exacerbated the hierarchical stratifications that had already existed: As large-scale farming, particularly with animal husbandry, emerged, it was largely men's work and its fruits were their property, creating patriarchal societies that gave supremacy to men and "male" values. The priests that replaced shamans, in turn, demanded grain as tribute to the gods and added institutional muscle to their predecessors' less formal and more ephemeral spiritualistic claims.

But for our purposes the most important consequence of the shift to farming was what V. Gordon Childe called the *urban revolution*. Some of the village settlements established by Neolithic farmers grew larger to become towns, and some of these towns developed further into cities—large permanent settlements in which the residents did not provide their own food but depended on grain imported from the countryside. For the residents of these cities, life was structured less around kinship than around residential propinquity and shared vocational activities. People lived alongside each other without necessarily being kin—ultimately without even knowing each other. In time, an outsider or stranger could join a community in a city simply by living there and bringing his or her labour to it, without having to marry into it or be recruited as a warrior. In fact, from a tribal viewpoint, a city was a place where nearly everyone whom a person encountered might well be a stranger.

To be sure, within early cities as in cities today, many people who were related to one another by clan affiliation chose to live in the same neighbourhoods as their kin or as a result of ethnic discrimination, were forced to do so regardless of their will. But the crucial point is that slowly, as city living became a way of life, kinship ties diminished as a principle of social organization and gave way to new ones. Lacking a shared ethnicity, people who were living side by side gradually came to see each other, not through the prism of tribal membership but through prisms of residence and vocation, status and property: as craftspeople or wealthy vendors, as nobles or priests.

Regardless of the specific category, the particularistic fetters that had locked people's forebears into tribal parochialism and intertribal feuds had been loosened. No longer were people of a shared genealogical background constrained to think of themselves as "the human beings" and of others as real or potentially hostile strangers. Ethnic prejudices persisted, to be sure, but in ever more diluted form than in tribal times, when ethnic difference alone could be a licence even to murder an outsider. The new social order transformed people from tribal folk into heterogeneous and potentially cosmopolitan city dwellers. The city, in effect, nudged aside genealogy in favor of a more ecumenical *humanitas*, or common humanity, as a basic principle of social organization and initiated the momentous process of creating human universality. As such, the transition to city life was as revolutionary as the agricultural revolution had been and as, several millennia later, the industrial revolution would prove to be.

The Emergence of the Political Realm

To be sure, these heterogeneous cities were anything but egalitarian paradises. On the contrary, the social relations that first replaced kinship were based on status groups, classes, and military and religious hierarchies as well as gender stratification. Ruling elites dominated the ordinary people who laboured to provide them with goods as well as mandatory military service. Priesthoods gained vast powers as a result of the era's ignorance of natural phenomena; early cities were often temple cities. Nor were cities—any more than tribes—immune to brutal periods of warfare.

Despite these tyrannies, the urban revolution opened to history the startling possibility that free and egalitarian communities could also exist and that people, once they recognized their common humanity, could order themselves according to rational and ethical standards. The rise of the city, in effect, inaugurated the development of the political realm.

It was the existence of shared concerns and public spaces held in common by interethnic communities in a city that made this development possible. Once they passed outside the walls of their private homes—that is, once they left the social realm—the stranger-residents of a city entered streets, squares, commons, and places of public accommodation—all of them places where they could interact with one another. Here buying and selling took place—and here also men and women could socialize. They could exchange news of general interest and discuss common concerns. The surfaces of walls could become places for public announcements and news.

Pageants and religious festivals could line the streets. Thus, public spaces came into being with the city—spaces that could potentially be set aside for civic purposes and political activity.

The Athenian polis made the earliest leap of transforming such public spaces into political arenas. Despite the persistence of ethnic fictions, slavery, and gender domination there, the polis defined and concretized the political realm as the arena of direct-democratic self-management. It also opened the historical possibility for political freedom—that is, the positive freedom of a community as a whole, with which individual liberties are tightly interwoven.

We will have more to say about the polis presently; suffice it to observe here that after its demise, direct democracy was submerged by the Alexandrian and Roman empires. Some of its features were appropriated for imperial propaganda, but its substance as a self-conscious program was all but destroyed. Centuries after the fall of Rome, however, the idea of civic freedom was revived when a number of towns in the Po valley and Flanders began to seek local autonomy from their ecclesiastical and temporal masters. These medieval communes shortly demanded civic liberties, including freedoms to make their own laws and create their own secular courts and forms of civic administration.

As in the Athenian polis, citizens in these communes came to manage their affairs according to their own secular criteria, not those of the elites that would rule them. In so doing, they revived the Hellenic tradition of the city as a locus of self-management and freedom. Embedded in an authoritarian feudal society, it is no wonder that one medieval Germanic adage had it, "city air makes free" (*Stadtluft macht frei*).

By no means, of course, did social inequality and ethnic hostility vanish with the rise of the political realm, any more than it had vanished with the rise of the city. From ancient times to the present, political elites have exercised authority over political life, even legitimating their rule by making quasitribalistic claims to ancient noble ancestry. In ancient Athens, as we have already seen, the polis was poisoned by slavery, patriarchalism, class rule, and imperialism. As for the medieval communes, even the most democratic were partly oligarchical, based on the rule of patrician merchants as well as master artisans; they were quasi-republics rather than democracies. The New England towns—another important chapter in the history of direct democracy—initially excluded nonchurchmembers from their town meetings, not to speak of women; moreover, the white freemen who populated those democratic meetings captured Indians and sold them into chattel slavery. Even during the most radical and democratic periods of the French Revolution, the assemblies of Paris were rife with xenophobic fears of foreign conspiracies.

Yet many of these failings were characteristic not merely of a given democratic moment in history but of the entire era of which it was part. Looking back from a distance of 2,400 years, we may now judge patriarchy and slavery to be repellent and inhuman, but Athens could hardly be expected to have risen above those basic features of ancient Mediterranean society as a whole. What is remarkable is that it did rise above monarchical authority and repressive custom, which were also typical of that Mediterranean world, and innovate a new political realm. Even as municipal democracies throughout history were mired in the hierarchical features of their eras, their liberatory moments sustained and furthered the tradition of direct democracy against ever greater odds. It is to these emancipatory moments that we now turn.

Chapter 3

Municipal Democracy
Ancient and Medieval

Let us examine some of the pivotal episodes in the tradition of direct democracy.*

The Athenian Polis

In the seventh century B.C.E., Attica—the city of Athens and its surrounding territory—was a scene of bitter class enmity. A tiny group of aristocratic families ruled the area, while the large number of small farmers lived as virtual serfs. These oppressed peasants were required to pay their overlords a large proportion of their annual crop, an obligation that often drove them into debt and bitter material want. As Plutarch tell us, the "common people were weighed down with debts they owed to a few rich men." For nonpayment of the debt, the consequences were often dire. "Many parents were even forced to sell their own children, or to go into exile because of the harshness of their creditors." In this intolerable situation the *demos*—a word that is used variously to mean "the common people" and "the people as a whole"—neared the brink of revolution. Despair impelled them to find someone who would "set all enslaved debtors free, redistribute the land and make a complete reform of the constitution."[1]

    Attica nearly exploded into bitter civil war, but eventually, in 594 B.C.E., all the contending clans agreed to elect Solon as their *archon*, or chief magistrate, to bring order to the polis.

---

*The accounts of the democratic moments given in this chapter and the next are necessarily brief, for reasons of space and proportion. In no sense are they intended to be full or complete; they do not claim to examine the causes of either their emergence or their decline. Rather, they are presented here to establish that this tradition exists and to describe some of its features. Readers who are interested in learning more about these episodes may care to examine the works listed in "For Further Reading" at the end of this book.

Solon proceeded to cancel all outstanding debts and make debt slavery illegal. Upon his election, in fact, he was given an extraordinary commission to alter the Athenian constitution and prevent new crises from arising, but the laws he promulgated changed the city's political structure so radically that, in effect, he forged a new constitution entirely.

Most consequentially, Solon revived the *ecclesia*, a popular assembly whose existence dated back to tribal days but had paled to insignificance in the intervening centuries. Under his regime, the ecclesia was not only resuscitated but its functions were expanded—as it gained the authorization to enact the community's laws, elect its magistrates, and meet regularly, at its own instigation. Finally, the new *archon* gave the common people the right not only to attend the ecclesia's meetings but to vote on the issues that were deliberated there, a crucial step toward empowering the *demos*.

In addition to the ecclesia, Solon created a new Council of Four Hundred—called the Boule–to handle the administrative side of Athenian self-government. To be sure, Solon was not an unalloyed democrat: he retained a certain elitism in the Boule by allowing only propertied men to belong to it. This elite prepared the ecclesia's agenda and supervised its deliberations. But Solon's Boule served at least to check the power of the aristocratic Areopagus council, through which the wealthy families had once ruled Attica as they pleased.

Other Solonic reforms expanded individual rights and established a popular court to hear appeals. In a further blow at oligarchy, the wealthy families were obliged to relinquish their hereditary claim to provide Athens with its archons, opening the door to executive power for the demos. But perhaps the most striking maxim imputed to Solon was his belief that any citizen who, as Plutarch put it, "in the event of revolution, does not take one side or the other," should be disenfranchised. It affronted the Hellenic concept of citizenship for a man to selfishly wait to see which side would prevail in a conflict.

Athenians were expected to be politically involved, to take sides during civic disputes.

Having made these constitutional reforms, Solon went into voluntary exile for ten years. Despite recurrences of considerable civil unrest, the citizens of Athens nevertheless absorbed his changes and grew accustomed to the ecclesia that he had expanded and empowered. They infused it with political vitality and developed a political etiquette that fostered civic commonality. Gradually the ecclesia came to be accepted in most quarters as the ultimate decision-making body in the polis, paving the way for a general democracy.

In the half century after 561, the "tyrannies" (not a pejorative word in those days) of Peisistratus and his son Hippias further reduced the power of the Attic nobility. In fact, many of Athenian democracy's features must be seen as institutionalized efforts to prevent the resurgence of the aristocracy. Although the aristocracy repeatedly tried to restore its old clannish oligarchy, it failed to eliminate the reforms of Solon and the Peisistradae; indeed, recalcitrant nobles were forced into exile and their estates were divided among the landless poor.

Meanwhile, precisely through their participation in the structures of Solon's constitution, the political level of the Athenian citizens was raised enormously, making them ever more sure of themselves and of their capacity to govern their own affairs.

The extraordinary opening of political life that created this self-confidence reached its apogee between Cleisthenes's archonship (beginning in 506) and the outbreak of the Peloponnesian war in 431. Cleisthenes, in fact, launched the democratization of Athens in earnest. Although he kept the Areopagus council intact, he struck at the social basis of aristocratic rule—the traditional kinship network of the Attic nobility—by divesting the clans of their powers and eliminating the traditional Ionian system of four ancestral tribes. In place of the old system, he created about 170 *demes*, units based not on kinship but on residence. In so doing, of course, he recapitulated the urban revolution in situ, replacing tribalism with propinquity as the criterion for membership and making citizenship inseparable from territory. The demes soon became vibrant multiple centers of local democracy, each one with its own popular assembly and its own council and other officials, all chosen annually.

This new institutional structure (which consisted of the demes and some larger units that the demes composed called *trittyes*, as well as a quasi-tribal unit that Cleisthenes kept in order to make the transition easier) revolutionized political life in Attica. The ecclesia—the citizens' assembly—was now indisputably the seat of all political authority. All male Athenian citizens were enfranchised and could participate and vote, free of property qualifications, regardless of class and status limitations. Their political rights were entirely equal, rich and poor alike, such that Pericles could declare: "Neither is poverty a bar, but a man may benefit his polis whatever this obscurity of his condition."[2]

Further constitutional changes made in 462 removed the last remaining traces of privilege from Athenian democracy. The Areopagus council lost much of its former weight when many of its powers were distributed among the Boule, the ecclesia, and the newly established popular democratic courts, where citizens sat in large juries, like miniature assemblies, for almost all civil and criminal cases.

In its prime, the ecclesia was an outdoor mass meeting of many thousands of male Athenian citizens, convening at least forty times each year, in meetings that usually lasted a single day. All could participate in open but orderly debates, according to the principle of *isegonia*, or the universal right to speak in the assembly; and all could vote, which was done by majority rule. Their decisions affected all matters of public policy, including war and peace, diplomatic treaties, finance, and public works.

Insofar as the polis had leaders, like the *strategos* Pericles, their terms were brief—usually one year—and their actions were constantly supervised and judged by the assembly, which held them to a level of accountability that prevented a self-perpetuating elite from emerging. But most positions were chosen by lot. In fact, sortition, rather than appointment or even election, became most widespread means of choosing officials in nearly all political institutions. The head of the assembly, who presided over meetings of the ecclesia, was not only chosen by lot but held office for only a single day. Boule members were chosen by lot for terms of one or two years, while even archons were chosen by lot (from members of the Boule), as were members of juries and other functionaries. That sortition could be used so extensively presupposed a high level of political competence on the part of ordinary citizens.

Such a presupposition, in fact, was eminently justified, for under this system a large proportion of the male citizens of Athens gained direct experience in democratic self-government. It was under this system that the city's cultural life flourished, begetting the well-known flowering of philosophy, drama, art, history writing, physics, and biology that constituted "the glory that was Greece."

The Medieval Commune

A millennium later, long after the demise of the Athenian polis, the Roman Empire had fallen and the feudal system lay like a dead weight over most of Europe. Although the Romans had founded many towns in Europe, they were no longer places of political activity. The church physically preserved many towns, but mainly as centres of ecclesiastical power. After A.D. 1000, however, in northern Italy, the Rhone valley, the Rhineland, and Flanders, a new merchant class began to emerge in the interstices of feudalism, and these innovators began to breathe new life into the medieval towns. Between the late tenth century and the first half of the thirteenth, the towns—or communes—that they revived became centres of lucrative commerce and craft production.

Initially the commercial and craft towns remained under the sovereignty of the older authority in whose domain they were located—usually the church or a count—and continued to be subject to external rule. But gradually the ecclesiastical and noble authorities were less and less able to address the local needs of the commune residents. Church laws, in particular, were irrelevant to commerce, when they were not restrictive of it. Ever more averse to complying with external control, the communes arrived at their own ways of handling taxation, marriage and inheritance, among other things, and developed their own legal systems, guaranteeing their inhabitants' personal liberties and limiting their princes' rights in fiscal, judicial, and other matters, until they were eventually managing their own local affairs de facto if not de jure.

Inevitably, the communes demanded that their sovereigns recognize their local liberties—demands that normally met with refusal from the ecclesiastical and princely powers. In turn, during the twelfth century, many communes began to free themselves from their sovereigns. In northern Italy a group of towns calling themselves the Lombard League rebelled against the Holy Roman Empire to gain their liberties. By the Peace of Constance, signed in 1183, the Empire granted recognition to the several towns of the league, permitting them to elect their own officials, to make their own local laws, and essentially to govern themselves.

What were the communes? They were essentially associations of burghers—merchants, professionals, and artisans—who swore an oath, or *conjuratio*, to respect one another's individual liberties and to defend and promote their common interests. The conjuratio was, in effect, an expression of citizenship in a distinct civic community.

The earliest communal institution of the Italian towns, in fact, was a general assembly of "all the members of the commune." This assembly approved statutes and chose a executive and judicial magistrate who, for a term of one year, was charged with the administration of town affairs.

As the communes grew in population and size, more artisans were needed to craft goods necessary for local use and regional trade, such as barrels and vehicles, and service workers were required to supply food and lodging. Rural people who gravitated toward the towns to seek refuge from feudal duties and to improve their living conditions took up this work, but before 1200 they usually did not share in the commune's political liberties. For the most part, the communes were not complete democracies; membership was restricted to the founding families and their descendants. Although all resident adults were subject to rule by the commune—they were required to pay taxes and to serve in the militia-not all of them were permitted to be politically active citizens. Active citizenship depended on property qualification, length of residence, and social connections, as did the right to hold public office, a right enjoyed by only a tiny fraction of the male population.

Indeed, in the twelfth century political power was developing along patrician lines, so that by 1160, in most communes, certain families were preeminent in civic affairs. Even as the communes as a whole were fighting for their autonomy from feudal lords and bishops, these patricians dominated the magistracy, manipulated the assembly, and basically ruled the city, with the result that the civic assemblies steadily atrophied.

This situation did not last long, however. Around 1200 democratic sentiments began to stir in many communes; at Nîmes, for example, in 1198 the entire people elected their magistrates. In the Italian communes the *popolo*—the master craftsmen, shopkeepers, professionals, notaries, tradesmen, financiers, commercial bourgeoisie (but not the weavers and labourers)—confronted the aristocracy with demands that communal political life be expanded to include their participation.

In various communes the *popolo* formed neighborhood movements of vocational guilds that interlinked men of the same occupation. These guilds were soon supplemented by armed popular societies, also organized by neighbourhood. The mobilized popolo now clashed with the nobility in towns such as Brescia, Milan, Piacenza, Cremona, Assisi, and Lucca, among many others. To a remarkable extent their revolts succeeded in radically democratizing communal political life. Between 1200 to 1260, in a number of communes including major towns like Bologna and Florence, the popolo actually took over reins of power. Pavia's council expanded from 150 to 1,000 members in the same years, and Milan's grew from 400 to 900, while at Montpellier the guild organizations actually fused with the municipal government itself. This dramatic process of democratization was reflected in the writings of the Aristotelian philosopher Marsilio of Padua, who wrote, "The legislator, or prime and proper effective cause of law, is the people or body of citizens, or its more weighty part, through its choice or will orally expressed in the general assembly of citizens."[3]

In the northern cities, by contrast, democratization of communal life occurred more slowly than it did in Italy. In Freiburg, after a popular revolt, the commune mutated its oligarchy into a board of twenty-four magistrates, elected annually, while Liège created a guild-type city republic and after 1313 made the issuance of new laws contingent upon approval by a popular assembly, composed of all citizens regardless of status. However, in Flanders, in cloth-manufacturing Ghent and Ypres, civic self-government was shaped by the weavers and fullers. Organized into so-called "lesser guilds," these working people—virtual proletarians—waged a veritable class war against their patrician exploiters and ultimately triumphed over them, establishing a civic structure that gave considerable rights both to themselves and to "low degree" guildsmen—and excluding most patricians.

Even at their most democratic, however, the popular communes of Flanders, the Rhone valley, and Italy still did not give equal political rights to all male citizens. They excluded the unskilled, the poor, field workers, and most immigrants, who, they felt, were dependent people and therefore easily controlled by wealthy merchants and aristocrats. Nor was the democratizing process long-lasting: In time these early democracies yielded to republican forms of governance, and political power reverted to the influential families, with the result that the communes later ended up with rule by oligarchical councils or by elites such as the Medici in Florence.

However incomplete the medieval communes' democratization may have been, it aroused the dormant political realm from its slumber and set it in motion for several centuries in piazzas and other public spaces. As such, these communes constitute an important moment in the developing tradition of direct democracy.

Notes

1. Plutarch, "Solon," in *The Rise and Fall of Athens* (Harmondsworth: Penguin, 1960), p. 54.

2. Pericles quoted in Thucydides, *Peloponnesian War*, 2.37.1.

3. Marsilio of Padua, *Defensor Pacis* (1324), dictio 1, chap. 23, sec. 3; in John H. Mundy and Peter Riesenberg, *The Medieval Town* (New York: Van Nostrand Reinhold, 1958), p. 125.

Chapter 4

❦

Municipal Democracy
Colonial and Revolutionary

The New England Town Meeting

The Puritans who settled colonial New England were neither willing nor conscious bearers of the tradition of direct democracy. The original generation who founded the Massachusetts Bay Colony in the 1629 thought democracy was quite frankly immoral. John Winthrop, the colony's first governor, and his fellow congregants much preferred rule by the elect, by the "visible saints," as they were called, who had supposedly enjoyed an epiphany of divine "grace." Scripture seemed to them to dictate that the elect should rule through aristocracy or monarchy.

Nevertheless the New England Puritans practiced a religion, called Congregationalism, that was remarkably democratic. A form of English Protestantism that championed the autonomy of the individual congregation against all priests and bishops, Congregationalism was based on the idea that each congregation of worshippers was an autonomous compact unto itself, subordinate to no mortal person, that was to be guided only by Scripture. Thus Congregationalist Puritanism rejected all liturgical and ecclesiastical aspects of the Christian religion—that is, it rejected not only the Roman church but the Anglican, which shared many of the hierarchical features of Catholicism. Congregationalists relied instead on scripture, on their own private relationship with the divine, and on one another, unmediated by clergy, for the salvation of their souls. Binding themselves into covenanted communities in the New World, they promised to obey God and to look out for one another's souls in a spirit of

31

mutual fellowship.

As they settled the Massachusetts Bay Colony in the 1630s, the Congregational Puritans formed fairly autonomous towns, structured around their own self-gathered churches. Each congregation governed itself by a covenant that its members wrote together as a community. An embryonic democratic ideal thus informed the ethos of each congregation: That the entire congregation participated in group decisions implied democratic rule, and just as each congregation had made its own religious covenant, so too did each town make a town covenant by which it handled its temporal affairs.

Their town-planning practices reflected this orientation toward democratic community. The original group who founded a town would collectively receive from the colony itself a deed to the land, which they divided among themselves. Each male inhabitant was given a one-to-ten-acre plot of land as a freehold, on which he could support himself and his family. Land ownership was thus kept roughly egalitarian, and extremes of wealth and poverty were avoided for a considerable period of time. The town militias, to which all able-bodied male members of the community belonged, were products of the same egalitarian spirit, as they mustered in drills on the town green.

As for town government, the New Englanders established town meetings—general assemblies—that met on a regular basis to conduct the town's affairs. The town meeting was essentially the religious congregation—with its insistence on a self-generated, autonomous covenant—reconstituted for dealing with civil affairs. Although the town meeting lacked any underpinning in democratic theory, it was astonishingly democratic in practice.

In theory only adult male churchmembers—those who had received "grace" and become "visible saints"—were eligible to vote in town meetings. Nonchurchmembers could attend meetings and participate in the deliberations, but they were not permitted to share in actual decision-making. But the towns quickly found that it was simply not feasible to allow only a minority to occupy the political realm, and the religious qualification for voting became a dead letter. The franchise was widened to include all adult male inhabitants who had some property or a regular income (20 pounds sterling, a relatively small sum), then finally any man who simply swore an oath to the effect that he possessed the right amount of property. The New England political realm was thus increasingly opened to men who would have been excluded in almost every English borough and town—that is, to most male heads of household. Moreover, anyone who could vote was also eligible to hold office. Contrary to the oligarchical prerogatives of England, officeholding in Massachusetts Bay was broadly elective rather than narrowly appointive.

The first town meeting, held in Cambridge in 1632, was a monthly meeting called in order to make decisions about local problems. Soon other towns were holding similar meetings, and they were doing so as often as they deemed necessary. In 1635 the General Court—the government of the whole colony—statutorily recognized the town meeting as the supreme governing body in each town.

At first, the townspeople themselves were fairly passive about exercising the broad sovereign powers granted them both by the 1635 statute and by their existing situation. Their town meetings assembled infrequently, only a few times a year, and transacted only routine business when they did. Townspeople preferred to delegate their power to the selectmen—the handful of officials who made up the select board, the administrative arm of the town meeting.

Nothing in the colony's legal code gave the selectmen greater or more powers than the town meeting itself—they were only supposed to carry out the decisions of the town meeting in between sessions. But in the first generation of settlement, the selectmen were religious elders or their secular equivalent—actually constituting a de facto aristocracy of "visible saints." As a small group of seven to nine members, the select board could meet more frequently and more informally than the larger and hence more cumbersome town meetings, and they could make decisions more expeditiously, without having to consult many different individual points of view. The townspeople could have voted the selectmen out of office easily—their terms of office lasted only one year but in the early years the people were still deferential to the venerable men who had guided them to the new land and formed their religious covenant. Holding the selectmen in awe, they reelected them indefinitely year after year and allowed them to exercise the primary governing power, while the town meetings themselves acted as mere rubber stamps, out of reverence for their higher wisdom and experience.

Between 1680 and 1720, however, the town meetings gained the upper hand over the select boards, transforming town politics from de facto oligarchies into de facto democracies. After the original generation of selectmen died off, the second generation did not command the level of veneration that their predecessors had enjoyed; merely by virtue of their relative youth the new selectmen were less experienced and less awe-inspiring. Thenceforth the townspeople gradually took the policy-making initiative back from the select boards. Instead of meeting only a few times a year to ratify the selectmen's decisions, the town meetings met more frequently—as often as they themselves felt was necessary, and they freely exercised their veto over the selectmen's proposals instead of accepting them docilely. They now claimed in practice the power that they already possessed legally.

Ultimately the town meetings came completely into their own as decision-making bodies. They imposed taxes, spent money, authorized land divisions, settled title and land use disputes, approved immigrants, granted economic concessions, and gave permission for creating various economic enterprises, functioning as the towns' economic planning boards. With the exercise of these expanding powers, debate and contention grew, and a new spirit of action and pride pervaded the meetings.

As for the colonywide government of Massachusetts Bay, each town sent delegates to the assembly in Boston. Early in the colony's history, the delegates, like the selectmen, had been elders, and their actions in the capital had been above public scrutiny. But in later generations the town meetings took an acute interest in making certain that their delegates voted in Boston the way the public at home had instructed them: An elected committee in the town would draw up a set of instructions to the delegate, then debate and vote on them in the town meeting, whereupon the meetings would bind the delegate to vote accordingly. Under the injunction of such mandates, a deputy became a mere agent of citizens in their towns.

As a result of popular pressure after around 1700, the delegates to the Boston assembly were required to bring an account of each session back to their respective town meetings. In fact, at least one town even sent a guardian along with the delegate to make sure he behaved in accordance with the public's mandate, and journals of the assembly were printed up precisely to publicize how delegates had voted. Finally, the election of deputies was annual—another powerful constraint on their power. (As John Adams would declare in 1776, "Where annual elections end, slavery begins.") By virtue of the towns' strong control over the assembly, the Boston assembly was less a legislative body than a confederal council or congress.

For much of the eighteenth century the Massachusetts towns enjoyed an extraordinary degree of freedom, a degree of sovereignty remarkable for their era or any other, by any standard. Although the "confederal congress" in Boston passed laws that affected the towns, most towns obeyed them mainly at their own discretion. In fact, disobedience was flagrant: in eighteenth-century Massachusetts the towns were supreme, not only on paper but in practice.

This experience with local power gave the townspeople an entirely new orientation toward authority. Long before the Declaration of Independence, the Massachusetts towns were operating on the principle that the only legitimate government derives from the consent of the governed—indeed, that the only legitimate government was self-government. It was the direct democracy of the Massachusetts towns, with what became their radical political views, that the British crown found most intolerable, and after the Boston Tea Party one of London's first acts was to pass a law shutting down the town meetings. It was an "intolerable act" that, given the self-sovereignty of the towns, could not supress their political practices, and their open defiance became a flashpoint for the revolt of all the American colonies against British rule.

In one of the ironies of history, the town meetings did not survive intact the revolution they did so much to generate; their power was eviscerated first by the State constitutions drawn up during the war and subsequently by the federal constitution. Although town meetings exist today, mainly in New England, the days when they were sovereign have long since passed into history.

The Parisian Sections

In France, the Parisian sectional assemblies of 1793 were the most democratic and radical political institutions to emerge during the course of the Great Revolution.

In preparation for the epochal meeting of the Estates General in Versailles in 1789, the French monarchy was obliged to establish electoral districts throughout France, where commoners could gather in assemblies to choose their deputies for the Third Estate—or rather, to choose an intermediate set of electors, who in turn would choose the deputies, so disinclined was the monarchy to allow even propertied commoners to vote directly. Sixty district assemblies were constituted in Paris, where they duly carried out their task. But once they chose their deputies, the Parisian assemblies persisted in meeting—even though they had lost their legal reason for existence. Thus, even as the Estates General—soon renamed the National Assembly—was meeting in Versailles, the Parisian district assemblies kept meeting regularly as quasi-legal bodies, acting as guardians of their limited freedoms in the fast-moving political situation.

After December 1789 such assemblies became the legal basis for municipal government in all the large French cities. The National Assembly, and later the Constituent Assembly that followed it, reconfigured Paris's sixty districts into forty-eight sections; all the other large French cities—Lyons and Marseilles, Bordeaux and Toulouse—were divided into sections as well, with assemblies to look after community affairs. Collectively the various sectional assemblies in a city exercised control over that city's central municipal authority, or commune.

As the revolution unfolded, about 44,000 autonomous local communes—the large ones controlled by sectional assemblies—occupied much of the political realm in France, concerning themselves not only with local but with national issues. They acquired the power to call out their own branches of the National Guard, and in both structure and political content, they became increasingly democratic and radical. In Paris the sectional assemblies even opened their doors to all adult males—and in some cases to women—regardless of property or status qualifications. Indeed, the Parisian sections themselves formed the basis for an extremely radical direct civic democracy.

This sectional movement, which matured in Paris in 1792 and 1793, was a self-conscious direct-democratic phenomenon. Regardless of whether its members were politically radical, each popular assembly formed the fundamental deliberative and decision-making body of its section. Ideologically, the *sectionnaires* regarded popular sovereignty as an inalienable right to be enjoyed by all citizens, one that could not to be preempted by representatives to national assemblies. Meeting in expropriated chapels and churches, each sectional assembly elected six deputies to the Paris Commune, one of whose major functions was to coordinate all the sections in the city.

Each section was also possessed of a variety of committees that performed such functions as police, supply, finance, and neighbourhood surveillance. Of paramount importance, each section also had its own battalion of the National Guard, including an artillery unit, over which it exercised complete control and whose movements it alone could authorize. The *sectionnaires* interested themselves passionately in these military units: assembly meetings in which National Guard officers were elected drew the greatest attendance, greater even than those in which civilian officials were elected.

In 1793, during the height of the Parisian radical democracy, sectional life was vibrant, disputatious, and earthy. Periods of crisis might attract a thousand citizens or more to an assembly meeting, often crowding the hall to the bursting point, while debates were often vigorous, the various factions contending with one another heatedly. Some sectional assemblies were genuine political battlegrounds. Within a particular section, citizens' interests might vary widely according to economic status, ideology, and social background—during even the most militant periods of the revolution, royalists and moderates still turned out for meetings, as well as extreme radicals. Furious confrontations often exploded into threats, shouts, and mutual recrimination, not to speak of fistfights.

The radical *sectionnaires* who occupied this political realm were the same people who invaded the Tuileries in August 1792 and deposed the king, leading to his execution; and who teetered on the brink of a radical insurrection against the Convention in June 1793. (Had it been successful, this insurrection might have given full power to a national confederation of sectional assemblies.) It was during this last period of ferment that the radical democrat Jean Varlet, whose political home was the section called Droits de l'Homme, tried to organize delegates from each section into a counterpower that would constitute a "Commune of communes," a confederation of cities and towns (communes) over all of France, to supplant the National Convention. In effect, the radical *sectionnaires* stood at forefront of the revolutionary movement in France. It was no doubt for this reason that their leaders were among the first to be arrested by the Jacobin regime when it came to power in June 1793.

Derived from the district assemblies, the sectional assemblies had elbowed their way into existence in flat defiance of the Nation-State that created them. They went on to provide the institutional structure for an extraordinary direct democracy, and as such they constitute yet another important moment in that abiding tradition. For libertarian municipalism they have a particular importance, since they were not only situated in the largest city on the European continent but played a driving role in radicalizing one of the great revolutions in history.

Chapter 5

The State and Urbanization

As familiar as the State is in modern life, its functions well known to every schoolchild, and as unmistakable as it is as a vehicle for domination, the State is nonetheless a phenomenon that is misunderstood across the political spectrum. Liberals and conservatives alike applaud its manifest custody of power, rationalizing it as necessary for maintaining orderly social arrangements, since human nature is, in their view, evidently flawed. Some go further to commend the State as beneficent, a civilizing force, even, in optimistic moments, culminating as "the end of history."

Leftists, for their part, have no illusions about the State as an instrument of domination. But they err in reading its specific features. Marxists tend to think of it as a mere reflex of class domination and at the same time as a tool suitable for appropriation and use in the interests of the working class—a substitution that merely perpetuates domination. Left-libertarians, for their part, rightfully reject the State altogether, but they commonly think of the State in ahistorical terms, as if it had materialized in the mundane world fully formed, a monolith without antecedents.

Like the city, however, and like the political and social realms themselves, the State has had a specific historical development. From a primal matrix of hierarchical relationships it issued gradually, taking a multiplicity of forms and undergoing degrees of development over the course of social evolution. Far from being monolithic, "the State" as a rubric encompasses germinal States, partly formed and unstable quasi-States, empires, monarchies, feudal States, theocracies, republics, social welfare States, autocracies, dictatorships, and totalitarian States. Like all

41

systems of hierarchy and class domination, States take a variety of forms, and their development has been, if anything, circuitous and fitful, multifarious and complex.

Many modern States are unitary in structure—that is, the power they hold flows unidirectionally from the capital. The localities have little or no power in their own right, essentially doing the bidding of the centre. The French system for example, is notable for its extreme centralization, in which local government is kept under tight control by the centre. A direct administrative link runs from Paris down through all the departments and *arrondissements* to even the smallest rural communes. Local officials are responsible to the centre and must carry out its directives. Even the construction of a new school in a small commune requires action from a ministry in Paris. This centralized system was bequeathed upon France by the Constitution of 1791; most of the European countries that Napoleon invaded adopted it in some version, whence it spread to other parts of the world.

The English system of local government, by contrast, has traditionally been much more decentralized, despite the aggrandizing process initiated by Henry II and Henry VII. Municipal corporations, antedating the Norman Conquest, were anciently independent of London, holding powers defined by charters and other patents. Counties, rural and urban districts, rural and urban parishes, boroughs, and county boroughs—all of these local jurisdictions were traditionally free from strict control by central authorities. Since the mid-nineteenth century, however, this tradition of local autonomy has been under assault and is now fast disappearing.

The Rise of the Nation-State

Regardless of how unitary or decentralized a State is, it is likely to coexist uneasily with municipal autonomy—with cities and towns that enjoy liberties of any significance. Even in the days of the Roman Empire, the emperor Augustus and his heirs made the suppression of municipal autonomy a centrepiece of imperial administration. They provided cities with just enough freedom to police themselves and to extract tribute from subject populations but with little more. Many centuries later, European princes and monarchs took much the same approach, curtailing municipal freedom where they could in order to consolidate their own power.

Indeed, it was essential to the rise of the Nation-State that the power of localities be attenuated and particularly that fairly autonomous cities be subjugated to the State's bureaucratic, police, and military forces. The centre first penetrated the localities by establishing unified legal systems over formerly diverse areas. In twelfth-century England, for example, circuit-riding "king's judges" spread the common law over the fragmentary feudal jurisdictions; under Henry II the system was expanded to encompass both civil and criminal cases, a rationalized system of trials, punishments and juries, and a professional royal judiciary. On the continent, kings and princes imposed Roman legal codes over broad areas in an attempt to clear away thickets of local legal conventions—and thereby weaken the sovereignty of localities.

Legal unification was backed up by force when royal States overran localities and incorporated them, imposing administration from the centre. Even the most ordinary rulers in the early modern period used military force to extend their command. But absolute monarchs in England and France collected enormous power into their own hands, carving out large-scale States from free cities, confederations of localities, and a multiplicity of feudal domains.

While central authorities tried to limit the power of local feudal lords, they also restricted the freedoms of vibrant municipalities that impeded the exercise of their absolutism. In sixteenth-century Italy, Machiavelli cynically advised the State-building "prince," the ruler or monarch seeking dominion, that it is harder to conquer cities that have a history of liberty and self-government than those that are already accustomed to princely domination.

French kings and their ministers shared Machiavelli's attitude, as the French State engrossed itself at the expense of municipal liberty. In 1463 Louis XI asserted his right to change any town constitution at his own pleasure, "without anyone doing more than watching," while Louis XIII and Richelieu had a fixed policy of "tearing down the city walls." During the French Revolution the Jacobin government made no break with this centralizing impetus: As we have seen, the Constitution of 1791 created the departments, overriding valuable local political features, while in 1793-94 the Robespierrist Committee of Public Safety all but quashed the municipal institutions of revolutionary Paris and of France generally.

Increasingly, ascendant monarchical States and later republics imposed pressures and demands on the various cities that lay in their domains, encroaching on their freedoms and usurping their powers. As they built up larger and ever more efficient administrations, States appropriated for themselves functions that had traditionally been the prerogatives of cities,

> In truth there is no sure method of holding them except by despoiling them. And whoever becomes the ruler of a free city and does not destroy it, can expect to be destroyed by it, for it can always find a motive for rebellion in the name of liberty and of its ancient usages, which are forgotten neither by lapse of time nor by benefits received.[1]

not only in legal jurisdiction but in economic regulation, coinage, taxation, and even diplomatic relations. Meanwhile, the seemingly incessant wars that kings waged with one another had to be financed; cities, with all their commercial wealth, became prime targets for royal fundraising. In the process of squeezing cash from cities, monarchs expanded their control over them, a process that gradually stifled civic freedom. By the seventeenth century, the formerly free city had been all but swallowed up by the monarchical State and incorporated into its centralized structure.

Resistance to State Encroachment

Outside Europe, we find few political concepts that link the city to freedom in opposition to the domination of the State, or that attribute to the city its own political life, customs, and habits in contradistinction to those of the State. Asian cities, for example, were primarily centres of administration for theocratic monarchies, where State and city existed in continuity and few civic impulses to rebel could find expression. But the liberty-loving town centres of Europe spawned a unique notion of the city as the locus of civic freedom. Indeed, from ancient times to the present, the city has been a major antagonist of State self-aggrandizement and centralization.

In the twelfth century, as we have seen, the confederation of northern Italian communes known as the First Lombard League rebelled against Frederick I Barbarossa's attempt to reclaim his imperial "rights" from the Po valley communes. It was because the confederated communes defeated him in battle, at Milan, that they gained the 1183 peace that became the basis of their communal liberties. Meanwhile, in France, Nîmes, Avignon, and Marseilles, having obtained their liberties in the early thirteenth century, confederated themselves and curtailed the powers of their princes. Etienne Marcel, a popular leader of the Third Estate in fourteenth-century Paris, sought to build an alliance of towns that would, with peasant support, circumscribe and possibly eliminate the powers of the French monarchy.

In northern Europe many towns and cities confederated not only to promote trade and their common prosperity but to protect their liberties. Sixty to eighty northern German cities, including major Baltic ports, confederated in the Hanseatic League, which controlled northern sea trade for several centuries. Also commercial and defensive in nature were the two thirteenth-century Rhenish Leagues in what is now Germany. By 1300 most of the municipalities in the south German area of Swabia had gained the status of free imperial cities—that is, they were nearly free from control by the Holy Roman Emperor, Charles IV, and other territorial lords, who nonetheless still claimed authority over them. In a further act of defiance, in 1384, they formed the first Swabian League (the Schwäbische Städtebund), without imperial sanction. As for the Netherlands, in the fourteenth century the Flemish communes joined forces in revolt against their overlords, while two centuries later the Dutch cities and their Stadtholders united to overthrow Spanish rule and lay the foundations for a Dutch Confederation.

In fact, as recently as the nineteenth century, it was still unclear that the Nation-State, rather than the confederation, would define the contours of power in Europe. Federative formations still abounded in central and southern Europe. The delay in the creation of Italian and German Nation-States was due in great measure to obstacles imposed by cities and their-confederacies, and although localist parochialism was also a factor, so was the strong tradition of municipal autonomy and resistance to centralization.

To this day, resistance to State authority continues to be nourished by village, neighbourhood, and town community networks. It the 1960s the Madrid Citizens' Movement, structured entirely around neighbourhood groups and institutions, played a major role in weakening the Franco regime. In the late 1980s the tremors that brought the Soviet Union to collapse were produced in part by movements for regional and local autonomy. When communal movements are on the upsurge, the instability of the Nation-State comes to the foreground.

Urbanization

Today the municipality is threatened by forces whose power

the rebellious and autonomy-seeking towns of previous centuries could not have imagined. Urbanization—the immense, formless blight of capitalism—is swallowing up the definable, humanly scaled entities that were once cities. Small communities are being absorbed by larger ones, cities by metropolises, and metropolises by huge agglomerations in megalopolitan belts. Sprawl, condominium subdivisions, highways, faceless shopping centers, parking lots, and industrial parks are sweeping ever further into the countryside as well. Such urbanization bodes ill for the liberatory potential of the cities, let alone for their persistence as the taproots of direct democracy. Indeed, urbanization is poised to complete the task that the Roman caesars, the absolute monarchs, and the "bourgeois" republics undertook long ago: the destruction of the political realm.

Today, as we have seen, people in North America and Europe are already losing a sense of the meaning of citizenship, and of politics as the practice of democratic community self-management; but they may also be losing sight of the meaning of the city as such. Indeed, the management of a city is coming ever more to resemble the management of a business corporation. A city is now considered successful if it simply earns fiscal surpluses and provides the physical infrastructure required to promote the growth of corporations. It is considered a failure if it is burdened by deficits and otherwise operates inefficiently by commercial and industrial standards. The *ethical* content of city life is being replaced by entrepreneurial considerations that emphasize the "bottom line"—to spur and enhance "growth"—that is, to accelerate the influx of capital, thereby increasing the local tax base, and in general to promote mindless urban expansion. As such, the very foundations for civic democracy are placed at the greatest risk.

The Civic Response

In the United States the decline of the civic sphere is the subject of considerable hand-wringing by commentators from across the entire political spectrum. Liberals and conservatives alike cast a fond, regretful eye back to a time when Americans were more community oriented and politically active, more informed about and concerned for public affairs. They rue the loss of the tendency remarked upon by Tocqueville in 1832,for Americans to form civic and neighbourhood "associations"— that is, to create civic groups, neighbourhood associations, clubs, and the like. Where liberals blame the untrammeled power of corporations for this loss, conservatives blame the tyranny of the centralized state.

Libertarian municipalism also regrets the diminuation of the public sphere—at the local level, of the political realm. But it does holds neither capitalism nor the Nation-State alone responsible for the loss; rather, both together are responsible, since they are parts of the same system. The State, as we have seen, was undermining municipal freedoms long before capitalism rose to ascendancy, and it continues to do so by eviscerating community life in favor of bureaucracy. But capitalism, by corroding public activity in favor of the market and creating intense economic pressures on ordinary men and women, has accelerated the demolition of municipal freedoms to the point that they may disappear entirely from the face of Europe and North America. Their synergistic combination has decimated both community life and individuality, and at the same time has forced people to concern themselves with issues of material survival rather than expansive issues of community self-management.

Nor does libertarian municipalism agree with the remedies that liberals and conservatives prescribe to restore the civic sphere. Conservatives advocate devolving "federal" powers—that is, powers of the Nation-State—down to the "local"— that is, state or provincial—level, thereby eliminating central bureaucracy. Such a devolution, they believe, would eliminate the dead hand of the central government, so that the "free market" would be able to move its invisible hand freely and restore individual self-reliance and entrepreneurship. This solution is patently inadequate, since enhancing capitalist expansion only accelerates the destruction of the political realm.

Liberals, for their part, want to restore the civic sphere by encouraging citizen participation in State processes. They would like citizens to vote, to write their legislators on issues of concern, to participate in electronic "town meetings," to expand the use of initiative and referendum, or to institute proportional representation. Such means, they argue, would give greater State power to those who would use it to restrain capitalism. But this liberal solution is also problematic, since it leaves intact both capitalism and the Nation-State. It is merely an adaptive way to work within the parameters of the Nation-State, and to leave capitalism relatively undisturbed, perhaps endowing it with a "human face."

Libertarian municipalism, by contrast, is a revolutionary political philosophy that aims to evict both capitalism and the Nation-State and to replace them with more humane and cooperative social relations. As we shall see, it starts with the residual political realm at the local level, working to revive it and to build it into a strong force in its own right, empowering people so that they are capable of ridding our societies of these destructive social processes.

Fortunately, the city as a site of resistance has not yet been entirely obliterated. Submerged as it is within an urbanized Nation-State beholden to capitalism, the city nonetheless lingers as a historic presence, a repository of longstanding traditions, sentiments, and impulses. It harbours memories of an ancient freedom, of erstwhile self-management, of a long-ago civic liberty for which the oppressed have struggled over centuries of social development.

That such traditions, such recollections linger in itself represents a challenge to the Nation-State. The municipality, in fact, continues to haunt the State as an irrepressible site for political self-management. Thus, however much the free community and direct democracy have been eroded by the State, urbanization, and capitalism, self-conscious municipal political life perseveres as a latent prospect, a cherished possibility, a still unfulfilled goal of human emancipation.

Today, unfortunately, such memories are too often revived by the right rather than the left. In the late 1980s a chauvinistic Lombard League sprang up in northern Italy, shrewdly trumpeting calls for dismembering the Italian State in favour of regional autonomy. Not coincidentally, the League also sought to end the flow of money that the State channeled from the north—by far Italy's richest area—to the poorer southern part of the country. The movement hearkened back to the medieval confederation of Po valley cities that defeated the emperor Barbarossa—although this time the presumed enemy lay not across the Alps but in the other parts of Italy (which may be the reason the League quickly changed its name from the Lombard League to the Northern League). But it is a sad commentary on the condition of the libertarian left that its once-cherished notions of municipal communalism and confederalism have been coopted—and warped—by the right, in the service of reactionary ends.

Libertarian municipalism is not a taxpayers' revolt; it is not a ploy for allowing the wealthy towns and cities to shed the burden of paying taxes to support poorer towns and cities. On the contrary, as we shall see, it seeks to eliminate altogether the disparities in wealth between rich and poor areas.

Today an antipathy toward central government is fermenting in many Western countries, an antipathy that takes many forms, ranging from mere skepticism about State efficiency to resentment of its usurpations of citizen power to outright hatred of its encroachments. Before such sentiments are once again exploited by the right, they need to be channeled into enlightened ends.

Unless the present competitive, accumulative market

society is to be accepted as the natural "end of history," the political realm must be revived and expanded in a self-conscious movement for municipal direct democracy. Here the tripartite distinction between society, politics, and the State acquires programmatic urgency. The political realm must be revived—or created, where it does not exist—and its democratic content enlarged beyond the limitations of previous eras, so that it becomes a living arena for change, education, empowerment, and confrontation with the State and capital. As the locus of citizen self-management and direct popular citizens' democracy, the political realm is the one arena that has the potential to oppose the Nation-State, urbanization, and capitalist society, and the blights they inflict on society as a whole.

Note

1. Niccolò Machiavelli, *The Prince*, chap. 5, in *The Prince and the Discourses* (New York: Modern Library, 1940), pp. 18-19.

Chapter 6

The Municipality

Libertarian municipalism is the name of the process that seeks to recreate and expand the democratic political realm as the realm of community self-management. As such, the starting place for this process must be the community.

A community comprises individuals whose dwellings are clustered in the vicinity of a distinct public space, forming a discernible community entity. This public space, whether it be a square, a park, or even a street, is the place where private life shades into public life, where the personal becomes more or less the communal. Behind their private doorways people enjoy the pleasures and cope with the demands of private life; but once one leaves one's doorway, one enters into a world where he or she is accessible to others, even as a degree of the closeness of private life is preserved. Here people encounter one another, unmediated by telephones or written messages, on a regular or occasional basis, and after repeated encounters they may become acquainted.

It is not shared kinship or ethnicity that makes possible the ties of a public sphere (although in some parts of cities people of the same ethnic groups may choose to live in the same neighbourhood). Nor is it a common workplace, from which people return after earning their daily bread. Rather, it is residential proximity and the shared problems and interests that arise in a single community, such as environmental, educational, and economic issues that form the underpinnings of a shared civic life. Encounters among community members are thus the germs of the political realm. The issues that community members have in common, as opposed to issues native to their private lives, become the subjects of concern in the political realm.

To be sure, people encounter one another on a face-to-face basis in other areas of society, like the workplace and the university, and these areas too have the potential to be democratized—in fact, they must be. Only the community, however, is open to all adult members qua residents, not to workers and students alone, and can therefore become a broad arena for the management of communitywide affairs.

It is from this incipient political level of the community that libertarian municipalism strives to create and renew the political realm, then expand it. Here people can potentially reconstitute themselves from isolated monads into citizens who recognize each other, are mutually interdependent, and as such are concerned for their common welfare. It is here that they can create those political institutions that make for broad community participation and sustain them on an ongoing basis. It is here that citizenship can become meaningful as citizens regain and expand the power that the State has usurped from them.

Libertarian municipalism refers to such potential political communities as *municipalities*. To be sure, the municipalities that exist today vary widely in size and legal status; they may range from a small village or town in a rural area, to a small city, to a neighbourhood in a vast metropolis like New York. But they still have sufficient features and traditions in common that we may use the same name for them. Their most important common feature is that they are all potentially sites of a nascent political realm where the tradition of direct democracy that we have been discussing may be reviewed and expanded. To bring the nascent political realm of any municipality to its fulfilment as an arena of civic freedom the governance of the city must be placed in the hands of its residents—the adult community members, or citizens. That is, it must be broken up and democratized.

Decentralization

If the political potential of the municipality is to be fulfilled, community life must be rescaled to the dimensions suitable for a democratic political realm. That is, existing cities that are of any considerable size must be decentralized into smaller municipalities of a manageable size.

Decentralization takes several forms, but the one that is most important at the outset is institutional decentralization. Institutional decentralization is the decentralization of city's governmental structure, by creating political institutions in smaller municipalities where now only a larger one exists. In a large city, it could mean breaking up the city government and shifting the locus of power and control from city hall to the various neighbourhoods. In a smaller city or town, it could take a similar form, except that the local units would be fewer and larger in proportion to the presently existing city. In a rural village, the size of the existing unit is probably small enough that decentralization is not necessary.

Ultimately the decentralized city or town would see the creation of a multiplicity of neighbourhood centres where there once was only one city hall; of new public spaces; and of a new infrastructure under the control of the smaller centres. It would see the development of local economic production. Green spaces could be created, where residents could cultivate food in local gardens. People who now spend hours commuting to senseless paper-shuffling jobs might prefer to spend their time developing their talents for carpentry or pottery or weaving or architectural design—and turning it into a full-time activity. They may find it more meaningful to join a healing or caring profession, or to educate the community's young people in history or literature or mathematics, than to sell, say, life insurance or real estate. Others might prefer to spend most of their time looking after very young children in whatever childrearing arrangements the community decides upon.

Decentralization would hardly require that all the institutions common to city life be replicated in miniature in each neighbourhood. Universities, for example, could be preserved as centres for learning; certainly it would be impractical to establish a new university in each city neighbourhood. Nor need major hospitals be eliminated in favour of smaller clinics. Nor would cultural institutions, like theatres and museums, necessarily be broken up and replaced with small theatres and museums in each neighborhood. But they would be removed from private ownership and returned to the control of the community where they are located. Moreover, the revival of community political life and a return to a smaller scale could well bring about a cultural awakening in the neighbourhoods, in that citizens might want and need to establish schools and healing centres and theatres and museums in their municipality, despite their access to the existing larger ones.

Even as institutional decentralization is occurring, *physical decentralization* could also begin. Physical decentralization is the breakup of a large city's built environment, in terms of its terrain and infrastructure. The smaller municipalities would need proportionately smaller city centres than the city hall, as well as smaller infrastructure systems, public spaces, and the like. New green spaces could be created near the centre of each new municipality, so that the new civic life has a focus. Not coincidentally, decentralization would also help rebalance the equilibrium between city and countryside— between social life and the biosphere. Indeed, physical decentralization would be indispensable to constructing an ecologically sound community.

Democratization

As decentralization of both kinds is taking place, the new and smaller municipalities would also be undergoing a process of democratization. This process of democratization, in fact, would be inseparable from decentralization. Here the new, smaller municipalities would become the sites of direct democracies.

The institutional structure of these direct democracies would be citizens' assemblies—large general meetings in which all the citizens of a given area meet, deliberate, and make decisions on matters of common concern. These assemblies would partake of the most enlightened precepts and practices established by their predecessors in the tradition of direct democracy—the ecclesia in ancient Athens, the *conjuratio* and the assemblies in the medieval communes, the town meetings in New England, and the sectional assemblies in Paris—as well as other instances of direct democracy, from any part of the world, regardless of whether they were indigenous to a particular region's history and traditions.

Of course, the citizens who create these assemblies would not use the ecclesia, the town meeting, and so on as models or blueprints. That would mean incorporating, rather than throwing into the dustbin of history, hierarchies of ethnicity, race, gender, and the like, as well as the accompanying prejudices. Rather, the citizens would look at their predecessors primarily for their specific democratic political institutions— and they would advance them further by opening them to the participation of all adults.

The assemblies would meet at regular intervals, perhaps every month at first, and later weekly, with additional meetings as citizens saw fit. They could meet in an auditorium, theatre, courtyard, hall, park, or even a church—indeed, in any local facility that was sufficiently large to hold all the concerned citizens of the municipality. The workings of the assembly would follow the canons of political decorum that are fair to all and allow the widest possible participation, yet at the same time keep the length of meetings within an agreed and reasonable time frame.

One of the first actions of an assembly would be to constitute itself—that is, to define itself, and to draw up a set of bylaws by which it will conduct its proceedings. These bylaws would establish decision-making procedures and offices, as well as the means of selecting the individuals who will hold those offices and the means of holding them accountable to the assembly as a whole. The bylaws could also establish consultative and administrative neighbourhood committees, councils, and boards to study and make recommendations on various issues and to enforce the assemblies' policies. They and their work would be under the continual review of the assembly, and their members would be subject to immediate recall. That is to say, if the members violated any of the community rules concerning the powers of councils and boards, the citizens would have the right to deprive them of their office and choose replacements for them.

In advance of each meeting an agenda would be drawn up, made up of items and issues that citizens have asked the assembly to consider. The agenda would be announced well before the meeting, at least several days in advance, in order to give citizens the time to marshal whatever contribution they would like to make to the discussion of a specific issue. At a given meeting, each issue on the agenda would be debated, in the presence of the assembled citizens. All sides of an issue, arguments and counterarguments, would be aired as thoroughly as possible. Indeed, a direct-democratic society that fulfilled the promise of freedom would not only permit debate, it would foster it. Its political institutions would be ongoing discussion forums, and its assemblies and media would be open to the fullest expression of all points of view.

To assure that different points of view are heard, everyone would have the full right of speech before the assembly. At first, most likely, those who do not yet feel themselves sufficiently articulate would be satisfied that someone else who shares their view has expressed it satisfactorily; but after observing and absorbing the deliberative process as it unfolds over time, it is to be hoped—indeed, expected—that they too would gain sufficient confidence to speak for themselves. As citizens gained experience in presenting their opinions in public, they would become more articulate, more able to convey arguments that they considered to be of vital importance, yet also cognizant, if they were not already, of the need for restraint and decorum. After a given debate, citizens would vote according to their best understanding of their vote's consequences for themselves, for other individual members of the community, and for the common good. The votes would be taken by majority rule—that is, if as little as 51 percent of the citizens favoured a measure, it would be passed.

Decision-Making Processes

Many alternative people, especially those of a libertarian orientation, reject majority rule as a principle for decision-making because after a vote is taken, the view of the majority becomes the established policy for the whole community and thereby gains the force of law to some degree. Inasmuch as the community as a whole must conform to the decision, they argue, quite aside from individual predilections, majority rule is coercive and therefore inconsistent with individual freedom. In this view, as stated by historian Peter Marshall, "the majority has no more right to dictate to the minority, even a minority of one, than the minority to the majority."[1]

The form of decision-making most commonly proposed as an alternative is the process of consensus, which, unlike majority rule, supposedly preserves personal autonomy. In a consensus process, no decision is finalized until every member of the community agrees with it. Even one dissenter can obstruct its passage. Such obstruction is all to the good, these libertarians believe, if the dissenter's own will differs from the view of the majority—such a person has the unconditional right to veto a decision.*

Consensus decision-making has its strong points, and it may well be appropriate for small groups of people who are very familiar with one another. But when larger, heterogeneous groups try to make decisions by consensus, serious problems often arise. By prioritizing the will of the individual, the process allows small minorities, even a minority of one, to thwart decisions that the majority of the community supports. And individuals will dissent, for not every community member will agree with every given decision; nor should they do so. Conflict is endemic to politics, a sine qua non, indeed a circumstance of its existence, and dissenters are (fortunately) ever-present. Some individuals will always feel that a particular decision is not beneficial, either to their own interests or to the public good.

But communities that govern themselves by a consensus process often reach consensus by manipulating dissidents into going along with the majority position, or even coercing them sub rosa, using psychological pressure or making discreet threats. This type of coercion may not happen in public view— it could, and often does, happen outside the scrutiny of assembly. But it would be no less coercive for that, and it would be more pernicious.

When the issue in question comes up for a vote, the coerced or manipulated dissenters tend to let themselves go on public record in favour of the measure, perhaps to avoid offending the majority—despite their strong opposition to it. In that case, their very real dissent is no longer a matter of public record, a respected if failed effort. Indeed, their dissent would be erased as if it had never existed, much to the detriment of the group's political development.

Alternatively, if dissenters cannot be pressured to

*Some consensus processes require less than unanimity—perhaps 80 percent agreement— in order to make a decision. But many of the problems discussed here remain. It is still dubious, for example, that 21 percent of a voting body should routinely be able to obstruct the view of the majority. In many instances this has meant that no decision was made at all because complete consensus could not be achieved.

change their vote, they may be successfully pressured into declining to vote at all. That is, they may "choose" to withdraw from the decision-making process on that issue—to "stand aside," in the jargon of the consensus procedure. But this choice, in effect, nullifies the dissenter as a political being. It resolves the problem of dissent essentially by removing the dissenter from the political sphere and eliminating the dissenting view from the forum of ideas.

By insisting on unanimous agreement, consensus either intensifies conflict to the point of fracturing the community, or else it silences dissent altogether. Rather than respect minorities, it mutes them. A far more honourable and morally healthy way of handling dissent is to allow dissidents to vote openly, with high visibility, in accordance with their beliefs, with the prospect of altering the decision in the future and potentially fostering the political development of the community.

In a community where decisions are made by majority rule, the minority does indeed have to conform to the decision of the majority, lest social life disintegrate into a cacophony of fractious individuals. But the minority retains the crucial freedom to try to overturn the decision. It is free to openly and persistently articulate its reasoned disagreements in an orderly manner to the other community members, in order to try to persuade them to reconsider the decision. By dissenting, even passionately, the minority keeps an issue alive and lays the groundwork for altering a bad decision and becoming the majority in its own right, hopefully advancing the political consciousness of the community.

Dissenters will and should always exist in a free society, if it is not to sink into stagnation; at issue here is whether they will have the freedom to express their dissent. Democratic decision-making—by majority rule—assures dissenters of that freedom, inscribing their dissent in the community records as public testimony to their position.

Note
1. Peter Marshall, *Demanding the Impossible: A History of Anarchism* (London: HarperCollins, 1992), p. 22.

Chapter 7

Building a Movement

If the political realm is to be reclaimed by the people in a municipality, if assemblies are to be formed and citizens empowered, then these goals must be pursued and fought for in a conscious endeavour. They will not be achieved as a result of accommodating oneself to existing social forces; nor will the powers that be hand them over to activists on a platter. On the contrary, today's social momentum may well be on the side of centralization and authoritarianism rather than decentralization and democratization. To educate and mobilize citizens and to establish those citizens' assemblies, a well-organized libertarian municipalist movement is necessary.

Nor will such a movement spring up spontaneously. It too must be consciously formed, and in any given community it must be formed by at least several people who are wholly committed to building it. How should such individuals proceed?

The first thing they should do is find each other and recognized their commonality of views. They might then decide to form a study group and use it to familiarize themselves with libertarian municipalist ideas as much as possible. That is, they could read the basic literature on libertarian municipalism (see "For Further Reading") and meet on a regular basis to discuss it among themselves, airing any questions that arise and looking for answers as best they can. By educating themselves, by preparing themselves for any opposition they may encounter, they will be equipping themselves to educate others and to advance the movement.

In addition to studying libertarian municipalism, they could also read works on themes relevant to it. These might include works on social ecology, the larger philosophy of which libertarian municipalism is the political dimension; on any democratic traditions in their own area or in other parts of the world; on the history of radical movements and on democratic and political theory generally, including anarchist works. They might also study works of social criticism. It would take a lifetime, of course, to master the literature that is encompassed by these suggestions; and it is certainly not necessary for the study group to have done so. Even after they have launched their movement, their education will be ongoing and will doubtless continue throughout the life of the movement.

Having given themselves a theoretical grounding in libertarian municipalism, the group then should go on to educate others. They should seek out friends and acquaintances who might be interested in the project, and expand their study group to include them. Alternatively, they might help to create affiliated groups, to which they could link themselves as the basis for a future political movement. By helping new people understand these ideas, they will also be testing their own understanding and learning how better to respond to questions, objections, and criticisms.

Public Education

When the study group members are confident that they have sufficiently mastered these ideas and are able to express them, they should work to become a force in the community in which they live. Before they do so, they should give their group a definite and recognizable name so that it may develop a distinct political identity in the community.

Their primary task, now and for the remainder of the movement's existence, will be public education, and a good place to start is the local political and ecological issues of concern to the general community. They should earnestly study these issues and take a position on them, developing a social-ecological analysis of them if possible. They should generate a literature on these issues clearly link them with libertarian municipalist ideas. They could write position papers, for example, or a general report on the all the environmental problems that affect their municipality, or on the likely social and environmental consequences of a proposed development. It would be invaluable if they started a community newsletter. Those who are more artistically inclined could make up posters and leaflets that call attention to a given issue and raise public awareness of it. Ideally, they should publish and distribute all their literature throughout the community, in local bookstores or neighbourhood centres or cafés. Every document they publish should bear the name of the group, so that those who wish to join it will know where to find it.

The organizing appeal that will have the most weight in their efforts at public education will be their call for local democracy–for the creation of citizens' assemblies in their municipality. The group might prefer to call such assemblies by a name more suited to their local traditions, but in their essentials they would be calling for popular direct-democratic institutions that foster democratic deliberation and decision-making.

The group should call upon their local city or town council to establish these assemblies legally by changing the municipality's governing charter to establish them, adding clauses that recognize the assemblies' existence and spell out their powers. Where citizens' assemblies already exist, the group should call for strengthening their powers.

As a further part of public education, they could hold lecture series in public spaces or in friendly cafés. They could deliver these talks themselves, featuring members of their own group as speakers, or they could invite speakers from the outside the community. The speakers might address a variety of topics, like democracy in theory and practice, or radical history, or current issues of community concern. If an outside speaker does not relate his or her talk to libertarian municipalism, a moderator provided by the group should do so, or audience members could raise it in the discussion afterward. Always they should emphasize the need for creating citizens' assemblies.

They could also organize actions around immediate issues, always tying them to the demand for citizens' assemblies to let the citizens decide. They might organize a demonstration to protest a development or the construction of a shopping mall, and explain the social forces at work behind that development. When issues of concern come before the local city council or planning commission, they should testify at any hearings that are held, and call for a direct democracy as a long-term solution. This will give them experience in public involvement, and at the same time spread libertarian municipalist ideas.

Very likely the group members will encounter or are already involved with cooperative endeavours in the community--cooperative food shops and cafés, communes, production collectives, and the like. These endeavours are valuable because of the role they play in developing a spirit of cooperation among individuals, which is necessary for the community solidarity upon which a direct democracy depends. But they are not in themselves libertarian municipalist institutions, since they are part of the social realm (see Chapter 2) rather than the political realm. Nor, given the capitalist system in which they are embedded, can the persistence of their cooperative nature be relied upon (see Chapter 12). Libertarian municipalists who are involved with these ventures should be mindful of their strengths and limitations and, while giving cooperatives their due, focus most of their energies on calling for citizens' assemblies and developing a vital political life and culture. (For more on cooperatives, see the interview with Murray Bookchin in the second part of this book.) Above all, the members of the libertarian municipalist group should talk to as many people as they can, to whoever will listen, patiently explaining why citizens' assemblies are necessary, repeating the same explanations over and over again if need be, and answering questions and objections to the best of their ability.

As the group attracts attention to these ideas and becomes a force in the community, it will attract new members. Certainly before inquiries become numerous, the group should compile a set of bylaws for its own self-administration. These bylaws would establish the existence of the group, its decision-making procedures, dues collections, and the like. But they should also establish meaningful conditions of membership. (It would not be undesirable, for example, for the group to establish a six-month trial period, so that new members may familiarize themselves with the group and its ideas.) In any case, to educate new members, the original group may want to hold separate educational meetings for them. It should certainly give over a portion of each group meeting to education—that is, to the discussion of writings relevant to libertarian municipalism and direct democracy.

Suburbia

A group that is located in a suburban area will encounter a unique set of problems that city and town dwellers do not face. In the suburbs public spaces are not plentiful. Unlike city dwellers, when suburbanites leave their homes, they usually do not step into a public space at all. Instead, they step into a private car, and they drive it until they reach another private place—a store, a gas station, a mall, or a workplace. They may go for days or weeks without entering anything but privately owned spaces. Sidewalks and other public spaces scarcely exist in suburbs, while community has all but given way to secluded homes set far back from the street, rendering chance encounters with other human beings highly unlikely.

Grounded as it is in the existence of community, a libertarian municipalist politics is certainly easier to initiate in places where people live in communities and encounter one another frequently. Nonetheless, although community feeling is far more diluted here than in a city or town, suburbanites also have serious concerns that they share with their neighbours and that require common efforts to address: concerns about environment, education, transportation, child care, and the local economy, among may others. Indeed, suburbanites are presently swamped with problems caused by pollution, inadequate facilities and corporate layoffs. The practical exigencies of life, in suburbs no less than cities, require that residents meet—even if they must do so deliberately and consciously rather than rely on chance, and even if they must track down a space and set it aside on an ad-hoc basis for that purpose.

In these areas the libertarian municipalist movement may try to arrange for public meetings themselves, putting up announcements in grocery stores, on public bulletin boards, in local newspapers, and the like. They may also help facilitate or conduct the meetings if the community members wish it of them.

Large Cities

Large metropolises present a different set of problems for the creation of a direct democracy. Sprawling urban belts like New York and Los Angeles are home to millions of densely concentrated people, most of them perfect strangers to one another even when they inhabit the same neighbourhoods. Such populations may seem far too large to allow for popular assemblies. In purely logistical terms, deliberation and decision-making would be so unwieldy as to be prohibitive. Even in a single neighbourhood, the number of citizens would be too large to convene in one meeting space. If all the citizens of New York or London ever tried to assemble in one ecclesia, the logistics would be insurmountable. Aristotle himself believed that a polis should be small enough to allow citizens to be reasonably familiar with one another.

Not only are these cities too big, but libertarian municipalists may conclude that their governments are so impersonal and remote that they are more like States than cities. Their city halls are run by elites—homegrown, to be sure, but still elites—and their machinations are impenetrable to ordinary citizens. Their election campaigns are as cynical and manipulative and corrupt as any national campaign. Once in office, mayors and council members administer enormous bureaucracies that do not lend themselves to decentralization. Transportation, sanitation, and commercial activities require a high degree of coordination on a daily basis.

Undoubtedly, the large size of these urban agglomerations does raise many problems for the creation of a direct democracy. But the rise of the urbanized megalopolis has not put an end to the historic tradition of civic politics.

For one thing, as we have seen, large urban entities differ from States in crucial ways. Not only are the respective histories of cities and States radically divergent, but city governments retain vestigial arenas for political life that are absent in Nation-States. Very often the inhabitants of a city—even one on the scale of New York—can intervene in community affairs to a degree that they cannot in national affairs. Municipal city halls, even those of big cities, are often far more accessible to ordinary citizens than are state, provincial, and federal legislatures. Neighbourhood centres are not difficult to create in large cities, while school boards and district meetings allow citizens of the same neighbourhood to meet and discuss common problems.

Second, decentralization will be prohibitively difficult only if the group members think of it in strictly physical terms—that is, in terms of territory and logistics. Such physical decentralization may well take some time to complete.* But institutional decentralization could be initiated at any time, in any city, no matter how large, and it could come to fruition relatively quickly. Popular assemblies could be started anywhere, even at the block level, regardless of the size of the whole city.

Once such assemblies are initiated in one or a few neighbourhoods in a large city, they could serve as models for other neighbourhoods, which could form assemblies of their own. The various democratized neighbourhoods could ultimately interlink with each other and form confederations that could try to coordinate transportation, sanitation, and other services. Neighbourhoods that are in the process of being institutionally decentralized to one degree or another could play a transformative role in the political life of the city as a whole and ultimately lead to widespread changes in its logistical and structural aspects as well.

It is conflating institutional and physical decentralization—indeed, conflating the end of a process with its beginning—that makes the process of large-city decentralization seem, prima facie, prohibitively difficult.

Even the largest urban belts comprise smaller communities that share a distinctive cultural heritage or various economic interests. Most large cities contain smaller cities or boroughs within themselves, most famously London. The five-borough city of New York is itself a very recent phenomenon, dating back only to 1897. As recently as 1874, New York City consisted solely of the single borough of Manhattan. Surely a city that is only a hundred-odd years old has not yet become eternal, contrary to what some critics of libertarian municipalism would have us believe.

Some large American cities have already undergone a degree of institutional decentralization. In 1975 New York changed its city charter in such a way as to strengthen its fifty-nine community districts, with their respective community boards. Los Angeles has had branch city halls for some time. Detroit, Pittsburgh, and Honolulu instituted a degree of neigh-

*Still, it could be done more rapidly than we might suppose, as the swift reconstruction of German and Japanese cities after the Second World War suggests.

borhood control in the 1970s. Anchorage, Alaska, adopted a system of community councils, while Dayton, Ohio, instituted six participatory planning districts.

In the 1980s the French prime minister, François Mitterand, tried to decentralize Paris by establishing local city halls. But perhaps the most dramatic example of institutional decentralization is the case of the Parisian sectional assemblies during the French Revolution. The population of Paris at that time was large—at least half a million people, which made it a megalopolis by eighteenth-century standards. Moreover, the logistical difficulties of city life were immense, as nothing in those days moved faster than a horse. Yet the sections functioned with a great deal of success on their own, partly coordinated by their delegates to the Commune, partly by confederating on their own initiative. In their face-to-face democracies, they not only dealt with political problems, they played a major role in provisioning the city, preventing the hoarding of food, suppressing speculation, supervising price controls, and carrying out many other complex administrative tasks and maintaining a militia that was the most formidable armed power in the French capital.

If it was possible to establish institutional decentralization in Paris in 1793, it should not be impossible to initiate it in large cities today. Not only do we have advantages of advanced transportation and communication, but we have an advanced understanding of the processes of democracy that eighteenth-century Parisians did not have.

Many large cities are already groaning physically and logistically under the burden of their size and are looking for ways to reconstitute themselves into smaller cities on their own. Most important, when asked in public opinion surveys, most Americans say that they would rather live in a smaller city or town than in a megalopolis—a feeling that could well make them receptive to libertarian municipalist ideas.

Chapter 8

Elections

It is highly unlikely, when libertarian municipalists demand that existing municipal governments surrender their powers to citizens' assemblies, that those governments will accede. Libertarian municipalists should therefore run for local elective office themselves, so that ultimately they can change the city charter to create fully empowered citizens' assemblies at the expense of the State.

Nor is it highly likely that libertarian municipalist candidates running for office on such a demand would achieve immediate victory. Their electoral campaigns would initially be educational efforts, to school citizens in the basic ideas of libertarian municipalism. All of the literature that the group has produced could be brought to bear in such a campaign. But for the campaign itself, a specific document is required: a political platform that summarizes the group's ideas in concise form.

The electoral platform should consist of a series of demands that represent the aims for which the group is fighting—above all the radical democratization of the municipal government through the creation of citizens' assemblies. But it is not enough merely to call for direct democracy; the platform should offer the steps by which that goal can be met. Indeed, it should make a series of clearly specified immediate demands, then place them in a radical context by tying them to the longer-term goal of fundamentally transforming society. For libertarian municipalism is a revolutionary movement, not a reformist movement, and it aims not to reform the existing system but to replace it with a liberatory one.

In programmatic terms these immediate and long-term goals can be called respectively minimum and maximum demands. Minimum demands are those that are immediately realizable within the existing system; they are specific and concrete. Maximum demands, by contrast, are more general; they comprise the rational society that the group hopes ultimately to achieve. The minimum demands should be formulated in such a way that they lead or phase into the maximum demands. Linking them in this way, the program should also contain transitional demands for the creation and expansion of social alternatives. Fulfilling a specific minimum demand, then fulfilling its more enlarged transitional form, should thus lead into the fulfilment of a more generalized maximum demand.

For example, a minimum demand to "change the city charter to establish citizens' assemblies" could be followed by a statement of intention to expand those assemblies to achieve the long-term goal or maximum demand of "direct democracy." Another minimum demand that the platform could articulate might be to "end the invasion of megastores and malls" in the area. The maximum demand would be to replace the market economy with a moral economy, one that is concerned with needs instead of profits. As a transition, the program could call for the municipality to initiate enterprises owned by itself that, as they expanded, could supplant the market economy. Another minimum demand could be to "preserve a wetland"; its associated maximum demand could be to "create an ecological society." Still another immediate demand could be to set up day-care centres and shelters for battered women; this demand could be part of the long-term goal of attaining "social justice" for the society as a whole.*

The electoral platform should always contain the group's name and contact information so that interested people may communicate with it. The platform may be used for public education not only when the group is running candidates for municipal office but at all times, in between elections as well as during them.

It should be clearly understood by the members of the group that libertarian municipalism is not an effort to construct a progressive or more environmentally friendly city government by electing "enlightened" candidates to the city council. Such a reformist direction would neutralize the movement's effort to create and enlarge citizens' assemblies–and its larger aim of transforming society. Rather, candidates should emphasize as often as they can that their movement's maximum aim is to create a direct democracy in their municipality and beyond.

The Campaign as Public Education

Those members whom the group chooses to run for local office should ideally be individuals who are most capable of articulating libertarian municipalist ideas and most comfortable doing so. For in the short term, libertarian municipalist campaigns will serve the continuing goal of public education, as occasions for the group to publicize their ideas and to spark public discussion. On every occasion—in interviews, debates, and speeches—the candidates should call for the creation of citizens' assemblies and advocate direct democracy. Candidates' debates are particularly desirable arenas in this respect, while leafletting door-to-door is an invaluable way to call general public attention to the platform and the ideas it contains.

The libertarian municipalist group should understand that its candidates are running for office not as personalities but as spokespersons for the ideas contained in the group's platform. It is these ideas that the campaign is offering to the public for its approval or disapproval—not the individual personalities of the candidates. As for the candidates themselves,

---

*For an example of an electoral platform that was used in a libertarian municipalist campaign, see the Appendix.

they are always accountable to the group for their political behaviour and not to the advancement of their own personal interests.

The best venues for the campaign are debates attended by citizens, where the latter voice their concerns and raise questions. Such events are occasions for generating the face-to-face political realm that is essential to a direct democracy. Media coverage may seem more effective than face-to-face discourse because it can reach more people, but the group should approach the media with caution. For one thing, it puts community political participation at a remove—it is no longer face-to-face—and thus vitiates the inclusiveness that libertarian municipalism seeks, perpetuating the isolation of ordinary people from public affairs. It also insulates candidates and ideas from the searching inquiry and challenge that face-to-face contact renders possible.

But what is also important is that regular commercial television news reporting is by definition biased toward the status quo and basically against the libertarian municipalist movement. While some reporters may be sympathetic to the movement, local commercial television stations will most likely be oriented toward the interests of their advertisers. Their news coverage when not entirely hostile could transform the libertarian municipalist candidates into media performers and degrade political discourse to the level of entertainment, offering only sound-bites and photo opportunities rather than thorough coverage. The group's best use of broadcast media is likely to be local public access television, which often allows for full, unedited, unbroken coverage of meetings and debates.

Electoral Failure

The present period of political reaction in much of the world will probably preclude immediate electoral success for the campaign, even in a community that is small and relatively pro-

gressive. In the foreseeable future, libertarian municipalist candidates will most likely lose whatever electoral races they run.
Least of all, in the 1990s, can a revolutionary minority hope to
gain rapid widespread public support. A considerable amount
of time may have to pass before the movement attains even
modest electoral success.

But in reactionary times such as these, paradoxical as
it may seem, electoral success is not something a libertarian
municipalist movement should focus on. Although they should
definitely participate in election campaigns, winning a campaign should not be a decisive matter. In too many instances
radical alternative movements have attained electoral success
before their ideas became part of public consciousness—at the
cost of their basic principles. They received votes because citizens agreed not with their larger aims but only with their minimum, often reformist goals; public education on their maximum goals for a rational society had not taken place. As a
result, a wide disparity developed between the political level of
the movement and that of the citizens. Yet the candidates, once
elected to office, were accountable to those citizens who had
voted for them, not to their movement's platform, which
inevitably attenuated the radicalism of their ideas in the interests of electoral "success."

A case in point is the Green movements that emerged
in the late 1970s and early 1980s in many European countries,
most notably Germany. Originally a countercultural movement,
the Greens were ostensibly bent on reconstructing society
along more ecological lines. In the early 1980s, Greens entered
the elections for the German federal parliament and won
enough votes to qualify twenty-odd members to enter.

The party rationalized that these new Green parliamentarians, suddenly thrust into the public limelight, would
use their State offices only as a platform to educate the public.
But expectations soon rose that the parliamentarians would be
able to pass progressive, ecologically enlightened laws—and

that they should actively strive to do so. But passing such legislation was possible only because it did not disturb the existing system; once achieving such legislation became the goal, the party was no longer radical. One by one, to increase the number of votes it received, the party shed its radical demands. The result was that the party was quickly absorbed into the institutions of the State. In the early 1990s, after the Greens issued a statement on capitalism that took positions markedly to the right of the Vatican, the principled left wing of the party finally left in disgust. At present the remaining Greens work entirely within the existing system—indeed, they appear to be eager to work with conventional parties, including the Christian Democrats, at whatever cost to their principles. Similar developments occurred in Britain, France, and Italy, as well as the United States, albeit on a smaller scale.

To avoid this kind of "reverse education," a libertarian municipalist movement must expect to grow slowly and organically and to patiently explain its ideas to ordinary citizens, educating them at every turn, without being deflected by the inevitable setbacks. It must remember at all times that its goal is not to produce still more members of the local governmental elite. Rather, its unwavering goal must be to recreate the political realm that allows for the greatest possible degree of direct democracy. To create that realm, the movement must educate the public and refuse to permit itself to be tamed by the State.

The story of the Greens may lead some libertarian municipalists to refuse to participate in any elections at all, even local elections. But local campaigns are a first-rate venue for educational activity. Despite the vicissitudes of elections and despite the potentially demoralizing effects of losing campaigns, participating in elections should remain a consistent and ongoing part of libertarian municipalist practice. As long as the movement adheres to its goals and principles, it will be building a meaningful alternative to the present society: a municipal direct democracy.

What libertarian municipalists should not do, difficult as it may be, is guide their activities by the number of votes they receive in any particular election, or spend long evenings contemplating and analyzing the percentages of the various contenders. Such preoccupations invariably lead to one of two outcomes: either to despair, or to desire for electoral success on any terms, as happened to the Greens. Rather than merely seek ever more votes from community members, the group should emphasize quality over quantity; it should be satisfied with a small but slowly growing group of highly conscious members and adherents, rather than seek a large number of voters who are only faintly acquainted with libertarian municipalist ideas— that is, a "constituency."

Only in a community whose political and democratic consciousness has been raised by the movement would it be desirable for a libertarian municipalist candidate to actually win an election. But when and if the citizens do elect a libertarian municipalist candidate to office because they agree with the group's platform, the candidate should remain accountable both to the platform and to the citizenry by immediately commencing the work of creating assemblies and democratizing the municipal government. He or she should aggressively introduce charter changes to create citizens' assemblies (or where they already exist, to give them increasing power, including the legal power to formulate binding policies for the municipality as a whole).

Libertarian Anti-electoralism

Many individualistic anarchists will object that such experiences as that of the Greens are endemic to any movement that enters into elections. They reject a libertarian municipalist approach precisely because it involves participation in elections, even municipal ones structured around direct democracy. Municipal elections, they argue, are of a piece with state and provincial and national elections, and municipal officeholders are qualitatively no different from officeholders in the Nation-State. Presumably, anyone who is consistently anti-Statist must reject local elections and municipalist politics.

Opposition to the State is amply warranted, but Statism is not the same thing as electoralism. Participation in municipal elections and city councils hardly amounts to Statecraft, especially when a libertarian movement is consciously directing this participation against the State(see Chapter 12). Cities and States derive from two entirely different traditions that have waged a recurring power struggle against each other—even in France, with its notoriously centralized State system. To participate in municipal elections—with the intention of democratizing the municipality and pitting it against the State—is to take the side of the anti-Statists in this ongoing struggle.

These anarchists, it should be noted, make no tripartite division of society into the social, State, and political realms. In particular, they negate the political realm by confusing it with the State, by accepting the conventional interchangeability of politics with Statecraft—a confusion that plays directly into the hands of Statists. The battle against the State, in their eyes, is to be waged by the social realm—that is, by alternative social groups, like cooperatives—and not by the political realm, whose very existence they deny.

Yet anarchism itself has always contained a communalist tendency, alongside its individualistic and cultural strains. Communalism holds out the ideal of decentralized, Stateless, and collectively managed "communes," or communities—in essence, of confederated municipalities. The orientation of this communalist tendency has long been municipalist, as can be gleaned from the writings of both Bakunin and Kropotkin. Bakunin saw, for example, that municipal councils are basic to people's political lives. The people, he wrote, "have a healthy, practical common sense when it comes to communal affairs. They are fairly well informed and know how to select from their midst the most capable officials. This is why municipal elections always best reflect the real attitude and will of the people."[1]

The political core of the communalist tendency, however, has not been sufficiently articulated in social anarchist writings. It is that lacuna that libertarian municipalism proposes to fill.

Extralegal Assemblies

In many places a libertarian municipalist group will find that the municipality has no charter, or that the city council or other municipal body consistently blocks its efforts to change the charter to empower citizens' assemblies. A libertarian municipalist councilmember may well find it impossible to persuade the rest of the council to legalize citizens' assemblies; or perhaps the community has not reached the stage where libertarian municipalist councilmembers can even be elected.

In such cases the group can create extralegal citizens' assemblies on its own initiative and convene them, appealing to all citizens of the community to attend and participate in them. These assemblies could meet on a regular basis and debate local, regional, national, and even international issues if they so desire, issuing resolutions and public statements as expressions of their views. To give the meetings structure, the participants should adopt a formal set of rules by which to conduct their affairs and establish them as bylaws. Finally, they could define the political powers that they ultimately claim for themselves.

Even assemblies that have no legal power could nonetheless exercise enormous moral power. As more and more citizens saw their significance and attended their meetings, the existing municipal structures might well have no choice ultimately but to give them a measure of legal, structural power.

Once this minimum step is taken, a transitional program of expanding the assemblies' power could be undertaken. As popular democracy matures—as attendance at assemblies flourishes, as citizens make these institutions their own—the assemblies would acquire ever greater de facto power. Ultimately the city charter would have to be changed to recognize this new popular power, to affirm that the assemblies hold sovereign power in the community. Thereafter the assemblies would work to achieve the maximum demands of a libertarian municipalist polity: the confederation of municipal assemblies and the creation of a rational society.

How rapidly the self-managed public sphere is institutionalized in these assemblies will obviously depend on the consciousness of the people. Much patience, it should be emphasized, will be required of the libertarian municipalist group, but its political venture has potentially sweeping possibilities for a broad transformation of political life.

Note

1. Sam Dolgoff, ed., *Bakunin on Anarchy* (New York: Alfred A. Knopf, 1972; republished Montreal: Black Rose Books, 1980 as *Bakunin on Anarchism*), p. 223.

Chapter 9

The Formation of Citizenship

4Liberalism, a political theory essential to representative Statecraft, posits as its irreducible unit the self–determining individual who, at the supreme moment of his sovereign power, exercises his autonomous will by choosing from among a range of options in a voting booth. Our society takes this individualistic vision with considerable seriousness, placing a premium on the sovereign person who relentlessly maximizes his or her self-interest at every turn. Such individuals are said to enjoy liberties including freedom from most restraints on profit seeking. Indeed, in American ideology, freedom itself is usually conflated with a heroic individualism, independence, and autonomy, as well as entrepreneurship.

Yet the much-praised autonomous individual is actually a fiction. No one can be autonomous from or independent of a social nexus, be it the private life that sustains them personally or the community life that sustains them communally. Nor is freedom accounted for only by notions of autonomy and independence, since these are mainly negative concepts of "freedom from"—indeed, of personal liberty as opposed to social freedom. Far from enhancing the individual's social and political freedom, autonomy subverts it. Ultimately autonomy negates freedom by destroying the mutual dependencies, the fabric of interrelationships, the civic and social substratum, upon which freedom rests.

Paradoxically, individuality, as opposed to individualism, gains its very flesh and blood from social interdependence, not from independence, since community support and solidarity provide the context in which the individual acts. "The most esteemed personal qualities," Max Horkheimer once wrote, "such as independence, will to freedom, sympathy, and the sense of justice, are social as well as individual virtues. The fully developed individual is the consummation of a fully developed society. The emancipation of the individual is not an emancipation from society, but the deliverance of society from atomization, an atomization that may reach its peak in periods of collectivization and mass culture."[1]

Least of all does an atomized society foster the active, mature citizenship needed for a direct democracy. In today's mass societies, as we have seen, citizens are reduced to mere "voters" and "taxpayers." Far from enhancing their mastery, the State and the capitalist system infantilize them. Conceiving itself as a paterfamilias, the State manages civic life on their behalf, presumably for their own good, but thereby perpetuates their dependence and subordination. At the same time, capitalism leaves no stone unturned in rendering them hapless, insatiable consumers, hungry not for power but for bargains. The citizens' very passivity, their very contingency to State processes, leaves them vulnerable to manipulation, be it by powerful personalities or by powerful institutions.

Mass voting in the privacy of a booth is but a pale substitute for an active political life. Here personal preferences for candidates are registered, tabulated, and quantified, like consumers' preferences in a market research survey, then processed in order to devise more effective marketing strategies for the next set of candidates.

In order to enlarge citizen participation and democracy itself, some observers have proposed expanding the use of "democratizing" tools like the referendum, in which people vote on specific issues. But referenda merely offer preformulated options; they do not allow for the collective formulation of policies or the expression of a broad range of possibilities. As with mass voting for candidates, mass voting for referenda continues the degradation of political participation into the mere registration of preferences. It debases citizens into consumers, broad ideals into personal tastes, and political ideas into percentages.

No reality could be more distant from the liberal ideal of the self-determining autonomous individual, in command of himself and his environment than passive consumers of paternalistic Statist options. Yet the ideal of autonomy is the prevailing ideology for in today's mass societies, deeply compromised as they are by the State, urbanization, hierarchy, and capitalism. As such, the ideology is not merely a sham; it is a cruel joke.

Citizenship

Libertarian municipalism proposes that passive dependence on an elite State is not, after all, the final condition of human political existence. A more active way of being is possible, it maintains, precisely because of some of the features that distinguish human beings as social, especially their capacity for reason, their mutual dependence, and their need for solidarity. Their independence and solidarity, in particular, can become the psychological, indeed moral groundwork for citizenship—and thus for the recreation of the political realm and municipal direct democracy.

Creating a libertarian municipalist society depends ultimately on changing social relations: replacing the State, urbanization, hierarchy, and capitalism with direct-democratic, cooperative institutions grounded in the municipal political realm. But its success also depends on the characterological qualities of the individual citizens who create that society.

Such a society would require a different kind of character from that of passive taxpayers and voters. Citizens who are active and innovative inhabitants of the political realm would develop a set of character strengths, civic virtues, and commitments to the common good that are either not widespread today or not much trumpeted where they are. Such personal qualities would form the character structure for mature citizens capable of democratic political participation.

Of these virtues, the most important are solidarity and reason. Indeed, the existence of the community depends on the community's ability to entrust its future to the solidarity and rationality of each citizen.

By any definition, citizenship presupposes a commitment to the public good—that is, to solidarity. In contrast to the cynicism that prevails today, mature active citizens would understand that the perpetuation of their political community depends on their active support for and participation in it. They would understand that they owe duties and obligations to their community, and they would fulfil them with the knowledge that everyone else in the community was bound by the same set of obligations. They would understand that precisely their common effort and shared responsibility were making the community possible.

Reason, another quality that is much maligned today, would also be of crucial importance to a direct democracy. Citizens' ratiocinative faculties would be vitally needed so that they could weigh the best course of action that the community should take to address a particular problem. Reason would be necessary for constructive discussion, in deliberations over an issue, rather than emotion-laden, visceral partisanship. Reason would be indispensable for overcoming any personal prejudices that citizens might have, so that they could treat all of their fellow citizens with fairness and generosity. Should an attempt be made to revive private property and an entrepreneurial, profit-seeking spirit, citizens would need reason to recognize why those efforts must be vigourously resisted, especially since emotionally compelling appeals would doubtless be made to their self-interest. They would need reason—as well as a great deal of personal strength and character—in order to be strong enough to uphold the good of the community.

This is not to say that in a libertarian municipalist society individual men and women must be wholly self-sacrificing and subordinate themselves to the collectivity. On the contrary, each individual would certainly live in a personal domain as well, with intimate family members and with the friends and fellows one chooses as companions, and with co-workers in productive activities. Indeed, in the empowered municipal community, personal relationships would probably be far more enriching than they are today, when neighbours often scarcely know each other and when the nuclear family, in isolation, must do all the personal work to support the individual, work that was once shared by the wider community and the extended family. The very condition of interdependence implies a degree of reciprocity among individuals. As fellow participants in a bold experiment, citizens rely on one another to share their responsibilities—and as they became more worthy of one another's trust, they would come to trust one another.

Indeed, individuality and community would mutually create each other. The communal decisions that individual citizens made would, in turn, would shape the social context in which they themselves lived. The political domain would reinforce the personal by empowering it, while the private domain would reinforce the political by enriching it. In this reciprocal process, the individual and the collective would nourish each other rather than be subordinate one to the other.

Despite the many differences that existed between them, the citizens of the ancient Athenian democracy, in general, perceived citizenship as the most authentic form of self-expression rather than as a burden of obligatory self-denial. They believed that human beings are inherently political beings, and that political participation is part of their human nature. They expressly frowned upon a politics that placed private interests before the public good. The collective recognition of duty and responsibility, shared by all, was underpinned by collective feelings of considerable solidarity and a commitment to reason. More than two millennia later, a version of this notion found expression in the maxim of the First Socialist International—"No rights without duties, no duties without rights"—that social anarchists and Marxists alike adopted as part of the ethics of revolutionary socialism.

Paideia

If State authority rests on the assumption that the "citizen" is inherently an incompetent and unreasonable juvenile whose affairs must be handled by professionals, libertarian municipalism assumes quite the opposite. It considers every citizen as potentially competent and reasonable enough to participate directly in democratic politics. It presupposes that, with training and experience, citizens can deliberate, make decisions peacefully, and implement their choices responsibly. It considers politics too important to be left to professionals; instead, it must become the province of amateurs—of ordinary people.

Such an orientation toward amateurism, as we have seen, was pervasive in the Athenian polis. With only a few exceptions, officeholders there were chosen not by election but by sortition—that is, by lot. Most officials were selected essentially at random, on the principle that every citizen was politically competent to handle the demands of most offices.

An amateur politics thus presumes that citizens have attained a high degree of political maturity, such that no elite of "specialists" is responsible for governance. The practices and virtues necessary for citizenship, however, do not spring from the human spirit *ab novo*; rather, like any form of civilized behaviour, they result from careful instruction. To some extent, children learn these practices in their families: the very young are often taught to give-and-take and to share, while older children may learn self-reliance and critical thinking. But for the most part, the specific virtues and competencies of citizenship must be consciously cultivated through a specific political education, which includes character formation.

The Athenians called this education *paideia*, the intentional cultivation of the civic and ethical qualities necessary for citizenship. These qualities include not only ethical virtues but a mature identification with the community and its values and a sense of responsibility toward it. Paideia imparts the reasoned restraint and decorum necessary to keep a civic assembly orderly, tolerant, functional, and creative. Such "civilizing" is what transforms a group of self-interested individuals into a deliberative, rational, ethical body politic.

How and where is paideia carried out? Academic study in the schoolroom is inadequate, while the mass media, far from fostering paideia, are capable only of undermining it. Actually, the school for citizenship and the character structure that sustains it is the political realm itself. Citizenship is created during the course of democratic political participation, amid a plenitude of discussion and interaction that engender knowledge, training, experience, and reason. In the very process of decision-making, the citizen develops both as an individual and as a political being, for citizens are the result of their own political activity. The school of politics, in effect, is politics itself.

Ultimately, however, the development of citizenship would become an art, not merely an education. Every aesthetic and institutional means would be used to turn the latent competence of citizens into actual reality. Social and political life would be consciously orchestrated to foster a profound sensitivity for the adjudication of differences without denying the need for vigourous dispute when it is needed. Cooperation and civic responsibility would become expressions of sociability and interdependence.

Citizenship Today

Perhaps the greatest task that the emerging libertarian municipalist movement faces will be to consciously revivify and expand the ethical traditions of citizenship and create a public sphere that can inculcate them. In our era of anomie and egoism, to be sure, the task seems formidable. The virtues and practices of active citizenship are alien to many people today. Cynicism about "politics" is epidemic, and any suggestion that one might put the "common good" before one's personal interests—let alone the interests of one's family—is likely to be greeted with mockery. Distrust of and even hostility toward "politics" runs very deep.

Yet closer examination reveals that the object of popular resentment is not politics but the State. Moreover, resentment of the State is healthy and legitimate, since the State represents a set of masters, not the common good. Unfortunately, so identified is politics with Statecraft today that for many people hostility to the State poisons their attitude toward politics. They become hostile to the very precepts that could empower them, that could replace their anomie with community and their social weakness with empowerment.

Still, the task of recreating a civic ethics may not be as formidable as it may seem at first glance. The very process of reclaiming citizen power and creating a libertarian municipalist society could become popular by providing sustenance for today's widespread hunger for meaning. It could endow privatized, aimless-seeming lives with a sense of purpose, so that people have something beyond self-gratification to live for. They could mobilize all their strengths and talents and in the process grow in ways they never could have predicted. The fulfilment of the movement's aims would create a better society in which their children could live creatively and with a sense of solidarity rather than with anxiety, passivity, and resignation.

The movement must therefore offer more than an electoral platform in opposition to urbanization and the Nation-State; it must offer an ethical ideal that not only casts moral judgment on the abuses of the existing society but reflects the virtues of citizenship. It must offer a replacement for the vacuity and triviality of life today, in the form of radical ideals of solidarity and freedom. Like the great manifestos advanced by socialist movements in the last century, it must call for moral as well as material transformation, with an ethics that sustains both.

Civic education and paideia are integral to the libertarian municipalist movement in all stages, from the study group to the municipal assembly and confederation. The movement should begin the process in its first discussion groups and lecture forums; in open discussions in cafés and restaurants, in homes, wherever people gather; and especially within the movement itself, at its own meetings. Here people inexperienced in political mores may become accustomed to airing their political views in public, in the presence of their neighbours, and debating them rationally. When citizens' assemblies are established, paideia will continue there, on a more formal basis, where responsibility and solidarity will become crucial in formulating public policy.

Precisely because it is conducted on a person-to-person basis, such civic education will make for personal interaction and trust—and the solidarity necessary for citizenship. Serious and ongoing political participation will help to eliminate prejudices and parochial sensibilities and replace them with cooperation and a recognition of mutual interdependence. As people become active citizens, they will learn or relearn the meaning of loyalty to their fellows, while their commitment to achieving success for the cause will deepen and intensify their courage and generosity of spirit.

Reinforced by ongoing political participation, paideia will intensify as the municipal assemblies attract ever more citizens, accumulate ever more power, and spread ever more widely into other municipalities. Still, these developments would only be a starting point. Serious participation in any struggle for social restructuring is self-formative and self-empowering. Having undergone a process of civic education, the people who begin the process of creating the movement will themselves have been transformed into more politically mature beings by the time they complete their work.

Note

1. Max Horkheimer, *The Eclipse of Reason* (New York: Oxford University Press, 1947), p. 135.

Chapter 10

❦

Localism and Interdependence

In the minds of many thoughtful people, the prospect of a profusion of municipal assemblies dotting the landscape, each of them making decisions autonomously, raises questions. Direct democracy and participatory citizenship sound very good on paper, they would concede, but the result of such fragmentation would most likely be not popular empowerment but chaos. Each assembly would probably try to advance its own interests at the expense of all the others.

Moreover, they further object, modern industrial societies are too large and too complex to be run by political entities as small as towns and neighbourhoods. Economic life in particular is interlinked and globalized; local communities could scarcely be expected to make informed decisions with the efficiency that production and commerce demand. By their very nature, our societies require government on a broad scale, lest they collapse altogether. The State is the perfect instrument for this purpose, we are assured—it permits policies to be made and enforced over a wide area.

Even those thinkers of a socialistic or utopistic bent who wish to replace the competitive market economy of the present society with cooperative ones may have doubts about municipal democracy. No lone municipality, they demur, however democratic, would ever be able to resist the pressures of large economic and class interests on its own. To arrive at a cooperative society, they maintain, a State would be indispensable—indeed, one with a great deal of power—to restrain the unbounded drive for profit of capitalist enterprises.

Still other critics object that small communities, by

virtue of their insularity, tend to become parochial. Even in today' s interlinked society, localities become complacent about their distinctive and cherished customs; but if their range of political vision were narrowed from the national level, where it rests today, to the comparatively minuscule town or neigh-bourhood level, then they might well withdraw into themselves at the expense of wider consociation. They might become reac-tionary guardians of local customs that are actually unfair or discriminatory. If challenged, they might become defensive of them, or even chauvinistic. A kind of municipal tribalism could spring up, one that shelters injustices or even tyrannies within.

The citizens of a chauvinistic municipality could even decide—democratically, in a citizens' assembly, voting by majority rule—that only white people could live in their com-munity. They could decide openly to discriminate against peo-ple of colour. They could decide to exclude women from public life, or gays and lesbians, or any other group. Without the power of a Nation-State to enforce anti-discrimination laws, these critics contend, civil rights wouldn't stand a chance. In traditional American politics it has often been the "decentraliz-ing" tendencies—calling for "states' rights"—that have stood for white supremacy and the exclusion of blacks from political life.

Finally, those who object to municipalist localism con-tend, environmental problems recognize no man—made, polit-ical boundaries. Suppose a town is dumping its untreated wastes into a river from which towns downstream draw their drinking water. Such a problem must be handled at a level of jurisdiction broader than the municipality. Only the overarch-ing State, we are told, with the instruments of coercion it has at its disposal, could prevent the upstream town from ruining the common water supply.

Rather than chase after hopelessly utopian schemes of direct democracy, these various arguments all conclude, people who are seeking to create a better society should work to improve the existing system—they should try to enhance popular representation in the State. To be sure, the Nation-State doesn't give decision-making power directly to ordinary people, we are told, but at least it gives it to their representatives. In general, even if the State is guilty of some abuses, it is necessary in order to prevent wider abuses.

On the surface, the Statist case may seem compelling. For one thing, it is true that today's world is complex. But society's complexity is not such as to require State control. Much of it is generated by the State itself, as well as by capitalist forms of enterprise. Eliminating the Nation-State and capitalism would immensely simplify society by eliminating their vast bureaucratic "complexities."

Second, while discrimination and other human rights abuses may indeed arise in Stateless societies, they may also arise in Statist societies—and have done so quite often. Nation-States have enforced abuses ranging from racial segregation to apartheid, from slavery to genocide, from child labour to patriarchalism to the persecution of sexual minorities. Indeed, human rights abuses have most often been perpetrated by States.

Finally, it is surely true that many social and environmental problems do transgress municipal boundaries, and that no single municipality can address them meaningfully on its own. And it is true that some municipalities may become parochial and transgress on the freedoms of others. Small is not necessarily beautiful at all, and municipal autonomy in itself does not guarantee that municipalities will be enlightened or free. Finally, it is true that the municipality is relatively powerless to challenge broad social forces—fighting in isolation, it would scarcely pose any threat at all.

The Statist critics, that is, are correct in their objection to localism as such. But although libertarian municipalism emphasizes enhancing local political power, it is not strictly a localist philosophy. It recognizes that some kind of transmunicipal form of organization is needed if citizens are to create and manage a free, democratic society. A thoroughgoing localism and decentralism, has consequences at least as unsavoury as those raised by Statists.

Localism and Decentralism

When most current radical-environmental political thinkers, for their part, turn to the problem of how to create an alternative society, they think of simplifying lifestyles and constructing simpler habitats at the local level that suit those simpler lifestyles. We should give up the pattern of insatiable consumption that society impresses upon us today, they argue, and reconceive ourselves as members of a bioregion—that is, a natural place bounded by a natural boundary, like a watershed or a mountain range. We should reduce the number of possessions we think we need, and society should cast off the technology that is (presumably) ruining the natural world. People in the wealthier nations in particular should drastically cut their levels of consumption and dismantle the technological base of economic production.

Instead of the shopping-mall society, we should frame a decentralized society, one in which our own "home," our own locality, becomes as self-sufficient as we can make it. We should build up local manufactures, using humble tools; we should create local cooperatives, like food coops; we should cultivate as much of our own food as possible; we should dispense with money if we can and adopt barter or an alternative currency. Local communities that are self-sufficient might then be able to survive on their own, outside the mainstream of society. Gradually such communities would multiply, creating a more humanly scaled and ecologically friendly society.

Such bioregionalist appeals share some points of resemblance with libertarian municipalism, especially in their objections to the competitive economy, to commodification, and to the creation of artificial needs, and in their wish to reconstruct society along more ecologically benign lines. And both bioregionalism and libertarian municipalism place great importance on enhancing the importance of localities, in that both call for the decentralization of society.

But many of these resemblances are superficial. While libertarian municipalism does seek to reinvigorate the local level, it regards local self-reliance as woefully incomplete as a principle by which to remake society and our relationship with the natural world. No locality—not even a municipality that practices direct democracy—can be sufficient unto itself. While we may strive to decentralize production, complete self-sufficiency is not only impossible but undesirable. Municipalities of all sorts are dependent upon one another, as well they should be, and share many common issues. Least of all should individual communities ever be autonomous in their economic life. Any given individual community needs far more resources, raw materials, than it could derive from its own lands. Economic interdependence is simply a fact; it is a function not of the competitive market economy, of capitalism, but of social life as such, at least since the Neolithic era. Even farmers and craftspeople are interdependent: farmers depend on mines, factories, and smithies for the manufacture of ploughs, hoes, shovels, and the like, while craftspeople need tools and raw materials from a wide variety of sources.

Nor would libertarian municipalism eliminate many existing technologies of production. In fact, it takes issue with the popular eco-mystical belief that technology is the cause of the ecological crisis. Most technologies are morally neutral (nuclear power of any kind is an obvious exception); it is not they that cause ecological destruction but the social arrangements, especially capitalism, that use them for destructive ends. Most technologies may be used for ends that are either noble or base; they merely magnify the consequences of the social relations in which they are embedded.

Certainly one noble end for which many technologies are used today is the reduction or elimination of toil. Those who advocate simple living, using only the simplest of technologies, seem unaware that if a "simplified" community were to try to produce everything its inhabitants needed, using only craft hand tools and simple farming technologies, the days of those community members would be filled with backbreaking toil, of the kind that was prevalent before the industrial revolution. Such toil not only prematurely aged preindustrial people, especially women; it allowed them little time to participate in political life.

Indeed, if people are to be able to fully participate as citizens in political life, as proposed, they must have a economic and technological base that will afford them sufficient free time to do so; otherwise the demands of survival and personal security in the private realm will overtake political participation.

Fortunately, creating an ecologically benign and decentralized society would not require a return to relentless toil. Social ecology (the body of ideas of which libertarian municipalism is the political dimension) recognizes that the enormous growth of productive forces in modern times has rendered moot the age-old problem of material scarcity. Today, technology has been developed sufficiently to make possible an immense expansion of free time, through the automation of tasks once performed by human labour. As far as production is concerned, the basic means for eliminating toil and drudgery, for living in comfort and security, rationally and ecologically, for social rather than merely private ends, are potentially available to all peoples of the world.

In today's societies, unfortunately, this promise of post-scarcity—of a sufficiency in the means of life and the expansion of free time—has not been fulfilled, again, not because the technology is base but because the social arrangements that use it are base. In the present society automation has more often than not created hardships rather than free time: it usually results either in unemployment, in which people are unable to gain the means of life at all, or else long hours of work at low-paying service jobs. An ecological society, by eliminating the social arrangements that create both these problems, would fulfil the potentiality of technology to create a post—scarcity society. It would retain much of today's technological infrastructure—including automated industrial plants—and use it for production to meet the basic needs of life. (Those plants, at a minimum, would be converted so that they were powered by clean, renewable energy rather than by fossil fuels.) Machinery would produce sufficient goods to meet individual needs and remove most onerous toil, so that men and women would have sufficient free time to participate in political life as well as enjoy rich and meaningful personal lives.

If the potentiality for ending material scarcity has been partially fulfilled by virtue of the development of production, that potentiality would be brought to fulfilment by making the necessary changes in the area of distribution. That is, the fruits of the productive forces would not be appropriated by one group, who then make them available to the rest of the world by selling them, as they are today. Rather, the fruits of production would be shared—they would be distributed according to people' s need for them, guided by an ethos of public responsibility as well as by reason.

Such sharing implies the existence of communication, tolerance, rejuvenating ideas, a wider social horizon, and cultural cross-fertilization—which would also help prevent the appearance of chauvinism and bigotry. But in an ecological society, sharing—equitable distribution—would not only be a moral principle. In order for the promise of post-scarcity to be fulfilled, it would have to be institutionalized; it would have to gain concrete social form through a broad principle of organized cooperation.

This organized cooperation would emanate from the

very interdependence of the democratized municipalities themselves, especially in their economic life, on ecological questions, and on issues of human rights. That is, not only would democratized municipalities be interdependent, they would institutionalize their interdependence in a direct-democratic way.

Chapter 11

❦

Confederalism

The broad principle of political and social organization that can institutionalize interdependence without resorting to a State and at the same time preserve the power of municipal assemblies is confederalism.

A confederation is a network in which several political entities combine to form a larger whole. Although a larger entity is formed in the process of confederating, the smaller entities do not dissolve themselves into it and disappear. Rather, they retain their freedom and identity and their sovereignty even as they confederate.

In an ecological society, the municipalities that have undergone democratization—that is, whose charters have been changed so that citizens' assemblies hold the supreme political power within the municipality—would form confederations on a regional basis to address transmunicipal or regional concerns. These confederations would institutionalize the inherent interdependence of communities, without depriving them of their freedom and sovereignty.

Instead of a central government, with a legislature voting to approve or reject laws, a confederation is typically embodied in a congress of delegates that coordinates policies and practices of the member communities. In a libertarian municipalist polity, the municipalities would form such confederations by sending delegates to them. These delegates would not be representatives; that is, their purpose would not be to make policies or laws on behalf of their supposedly benighted constituents, in ways that they imagine to be beneficial to them. Instead, the delegates would be mandated by the people in their municipal assemblies to carry out their wishes.

The delegates' functions would be to convey the wishes of the municipality to the confederal level. In conjunction with the other delegates in the confederation, they would coordinate policies to meet common ends that the several member communities have agreed upon and adjudicate any differences that may arise among themselves. All delegates would be accountable to the assemblies that have mandated them as their agents.

Confederations in History

Confederal structures, it should be emphasized, are not historically novel. To the contrary, early cities at the dawn of recorded history established confederal associations, as they did in the ancient Mediterranean and medieval European worlds. In early modern times confederations gained notable importance as a major viable alternative to the Nation-State, before the Nation-State attained the prevalence that it has today.

Insofar as cities have resisted the encroachments of the State, they have often done so by joining together to form confederations. We saw several examples of cities forming leagues and confederacies in Chapter 5, but two important cases that have not yet been mentioned are those of Switzerland and Castile, in Spain.

Today Switzerland, because it is still a confederation, seems anomalous among the relatively more unitary Nation-States of Europe. But in earlier times, in central Europe especially, it was confederations that were the norm and States that were the anomaly. Confederations abounded in the thirteenth and fourteenth centuries, like the Rhenish and Swabian leagues. Switzerland merely preserved much of this older confederal trend, while its neighbours underwent centralization to become more modern States. Its governmental structure is still relatively decentralized, made up of twenty-two cantons, which still have a good deal of autonomy from the federal level; in turn the three thousand communes still have some autonomy from the cantons in which they are located.

But Switzerland today also has many State features (as well as attitudes, institutions, and social features that are not at all enlightened). Swiss confederalism is far more interesting historically. Most strikingly, in the country's easternmost territory—which was once called Raetia by the Romans and is now called the canton of Graubünden—the Swiss communes formed confederations for their common welfare and safety.

At the beginning of the sixteenth century in Raetia, three confederal leagues (the Gotteshausbund, the Oberbund or Grauer Bund, and the Zehngerichtenbund) coexisted. In 1524 these three leagues allied to form the Free State of the Three Leagues, which despite its "Statist" name was a confederation. The Free State confederation lasted for almost three centuries, until Napoleon forced it into the Swiss Confederation in 1803.

All three of its component leagues, in turn, were made up of communes that were remarkably democratic and free. Indeed, the ultimate sovereignty in the Free State reposed with the communes, which held assemblies much like "town meetings" and would give their assent or opposition to a proposed course of action by referendum. They controlled their own judicial and economic affairs, as well as the local police and military forces. And they functioned along surprisingly communistic lines, using local resources in ways that approximated collective ownership. For example, they privileged the right to graze cattle communally. In a pastoral economy, common grazing such as they practised amounted to overriding private property and negating private land ownership.

The only central "government" in the Free State confederation was a commission consisting of the respective heads of each of the three leagues and an elective assembly, which together proposed referenda and carried out the will of the communes. The commissioners had the right to handle foreign affairs and to prevent the component leagues from making foreign alliances on their own. But the communes themselves decided upon matters of war and peace, as well as domestic issues.

The central "government" thus had almost no power, while the communes—that is, the citizens themselves, in assembly—had a great deal. In effect, the commissioners were merely attendants upon the people. Ultimately they lost to the communes even the power to handle diplomacy and make treaties. In general, the history of Raetia for these three centuries is a striking testimony to the ability of direct-democratic communities to govern themselves in confederal union.[1]

In sixteenth-century Castile, confederalism was part of a revolutionary struggle. In 1520 Toledo's city council called upon all the cities represented in the Cortes to establish a common front against the royal government, which had made an unfavourable change in its tax policy. City after city in Castile went into a full-scale revolt. They organized civic militias and democratized their municipal governments.

A national junta—the equivalent of a confederal council—was established, with delegates from all the Cortes cities, constituting a dual power in opposition to the royal administration. Mustering an army of citizens and adding to it professional solders, this *comunero* junta won military victories that threatened to replace the monarchical State with the municipal confederation.

The concrete aims of the *comunero* movement were municipal democracy and a Cortes composed of city delegations that would greatly limit royal authority. The movement's so-called Vallidolid articles demanded that Cortes delegates be chosen with the consent of the parishes—that is, by assemblies of the people—rather than by city councils. These delegates, in turn, were to be guided by the mandate of their electors and were obliged to take their instructions from their home cities. The Cortes was expected to meet regularly and address all grievances before closing.[2]

Had these demands been realized, Castile would have seen the emergence of a broadly based local democracy, one deeply rooted in city neighbourhoods as well as towns. After a demanding conflict, however, that included a siege of Toledo, the State prevailed over the confederation when the king militarily defeated the very popular *comuneros*.

Confederal Organization

In an ecological society, the direct-democratic municipal assemblies would elect their delegates to serve on a confederal council. This council would be a congress of the delegates from the various municipal assemblies. Like the commission in the Swiss example, the council would have little power of its own but would merely carry out the will of the municipalities.

Moreover, the delegates would be strictly mandated to vote according to the wishes of their home municipalities, which would give them rigourous instructions in writing. They would not be permitted to make policy decisions without their home municipality's specific instructions. Entirely responsible to the citizens' assemblies, the delegates would be recallable in the event that they violated a mandate.

Rather than making policy decisions in its own right, the confederal council would exist primarily for administrative purposes—that is, for the purpose of coordinating and executing policies formulated by the assemblies.

Policy-making versus Administration

Fundamental to libertarian municipalism is the distinction between policy-making and the execution of those policies, or between policy-making and administration.

At the municipal level, the citizens in their democratic assemblies would make policy. They would deliberate on the various courses of action open to them on a particular issue, then decide which one to take. Suppose an assembly was debating whether to build a road. After weighing the pros and cons of building the road, the citizens might vote that the road was necessary. Their decision to build it is an example of policy-making.

The road could be built over any of several routes. The engineers in the community would devise plans for the various possibilities, solving any technical problems that might arise with each, then bring those plans to the assembly. There the engineers would lay the alternatives before the citizens, explaining each one clearly. Few of the citizens in the community would likely know how to build a road, but then, such expertise would not be necessary for them to have. It would merely be necessary that they understand clear explanations and the differences among the plans.

Most important, the engineers would not be the ones to decide which road to build (except in their capacity as citizens). They would simply function as a panel of experts. After debating the strengths and weaknesses of each plan, it is the citizens (including the experts in their capacity as citizens) who would choose their preference. This choice is another example of policy-making.

Finally, the road itself would have to be constructed. Unlike the other stages of the process, the construction of the road would be strictly an administrative responsibility—it would require no deliberation, no voting. The road-builders would carry out the decision made by the assembly, building the road according to the chosen plan. This strictly technical process of execution is an example of administration—in which no policy-making is involved.

In a libertarian municipalist polity, as in our world today, many decisions require that the decision-makers consider a multitude of complex and difficult factors. But then as now, technical knowledge is usually not necessary for making political choices. Few parliamentarians today would be able to design a nuclear power plant or even explain how one works, but that does not bar them from making policy decisions about the use of nuclear energy. In a libertarian municipalist society the knowledge that is needed would be disseminated as widely as possible among the citizenry. Technical issues should be presented clearly and accessibly, so that ordinary citizens of reasonable competence can make policy decisions concerning them. Guaranteeing that all matters of policy are the province of reasonable, competent citizens will help to preserve a clear and institutionalized distinction between policy-making and administration, thereby making direct democracy feasible.

Karl Marx, in his analysis of the Paris Commune of 1871, did radical social theory a considerable disservice when he celebrated the fact that the Commune had combined delegated policy-making with the execution of policies by its own administrators. In fact, this merging of the two functions was actually a major failing of that body. When the people who are administrators come to make policy decisions as well, the groundwork for a State has been laid: An elite is in the process of usurping the citizens' decision-making power.

As we have seen, in the early period of the Massachusetts Bay Colony the select boards—which were supposed to perform only administrative functions—actually made policy decisions as well, arrogating for themselves the powers that rightfully belonged to the town meetings. When such administrative bodies are permitted to function outside public scrutiny, they can make policy decisions surreptitiously and cloak them as administrative or "practical" matters. Articulating and preserving the distinction between the two functions, however, will assure—as much as is humanly possible—that administrators make only administrative decisions, not policies.

Confederal Referenda

In the new city as envisaged here, policy-making would be the exclusive privilege of the municipal assemblies, of free citizens voting in a direct democracy. The functions of the confederal council would be purely administrative and coordinative, executing the policies that the municipalities have adopted.

One process that the confederation council would coordinate would be confederation-wide voting. Suppose again that one member community of the confederation was wreaking ecological mayhem (dumping its wastes in the river) or violating human rights (excluding people of colour). One or more of its fellow municipalities could propose that the all the member municipalities vote on whether that community may persist in its noxious practice. The confederation council would coordinate what amounted to a confederal referendum in which, if they so chose, the municipalities could vote that that community desist from its malfeasances.

The voting, by majority rule, would be tallied according to the popular vote, not by municipal jurisdiction: that is, each delegate to the confederal council would carry a tally of the positive and negative votes from his or her municipality. The aggregate votes of all the citizens of all the municipalities in the confederation would be added together to determine the final outcome.

Such a process would represent not a denial of democracy but the assertion of a shared agreement by the majority of citizens within the confederation that the ecological integrity of a region or human rights must be maintained. It would not be the confederal council that made this decision, but the cumulative majority of all the citizens in all the assemblies, conceived in the aggregate as one large community that expressed its wishes through the confederation.

On many issues, referenda need not demand an answer

of either yes or no. In today's referenda conducted by and for the Nation-State, people have a very limited choice: they may vote either yes or no on a referendum, as it has been formulated in advance. But in the confederation of municipalities, an assembly may decide, during its period of deliberation and debate, that it cares for neither option and prefers to formulate its own. In such a case, the confederated municipalities may eventually choose from a range of options presented rather than voting to accept or reject only one.

Assembly Supremacy

Even as they possessed the power to prevent a particular municipality from inflicting moral or physical damage on its own members or on other towns or cities, the municipalities would have the ultimate power within the confederation. It is they, collectively, that would reign supreme as the formulators of policy.

The principle of assembly sovereignty is what distinguishes the libertarian municipalist approach from Statism. A radical, anticapitalist party that captured the existing apparatus of a Nation-State but merely went on to reconstitute another State might well abolish private property and take over the means of production, but such a State would not constitute a direct democracy. Its power over people would undoubtedly grow and, if recent experience is any guide, become all-encompassing, reinforcing its State power with economic power. It would undoubtedly develop a large bureaucracy to administer its comprehensive controls. Whatever its success in restraining capitalism, such a Statist trajectory could well prove disastrous.

Consciously formed to accommodate interdependencies, by contrast, a confederation of municipalities would be based on the full accountability of confederal delegates, the right to recall, and firm mandates. As such, the confederation would unite municipal democratic decision-making with trans-municipal administration. Most significantly, the confederation of municipalities could fulfil the longstanding dream of revolutionary movements past, to achieve "the Commune of communes."

Notes

1. For a fine account of this history, see Benjamin Barber, *The Death of Communal Liberty: A History of Freedom in a Swiss Mountain Canton* (Princeton University Press, 1974).

2. See Manuel Castells, *The City and the Grassroots: A Cross-Cultural Theory of Urban Social Movements* (Berkeley and Los Angeles: University of California Press, 1983), chap. 2.

Chapter 12

A Municipalized Economy

The movement to create a libertarian municipalist society will face many social adversaries as it grows and spreads over ever wider areas. One of these adversaries, of course, is the Nation-State, that coercive power structure that substitutes a system of elites and masses for direct democracy yet has the insolence to label itself democratic. Another foe is urbanization, that warping of the city that further lays waste to the political realm by replacing the city and the community with the megalopolis. Still another foe is hierarchy, the various institutionalized divisions of humanity according to gender, ethnicity, race, age, and status, in which one group is endowed with the right to dominate others, often by invoking a mythic biological superiority as justification.

But perhaps the most pernicious and intractable enemy that the movement for fundamental change will face is of another order altogether. That enemy is capitalism itself, and the social devastation that it has wrought on human societies around the world.

To many people today, it seems incongruous to speak of capitalism as inimical to a good life, let alone as wreaking devastation. After all, at the end of the cold war, the demise of the Soviet Union supposedly proved that any quest for a socialistic or communistic alternative to capitalism is dangerously misguided, that it will inevitably lead to totalitarianism and environmental blight. Out of the historic struggle between the "free" market and its enemies, capitalism emerged triumphant, in this view; therefore, capitalism is morally right.

This attitude is in itself an indication of the scope of the problem that a libertarian municipalist movement faces. Today capitalism is increasingly perceived, as Marx once feared it would be, as synonymous with "the economy"—that is, as the economic order that best suits human nature, that comes as naturally to human activity as eating and breathing because it expresses an allegedly "natural" human drive to grow, compete, and win. So decisive, in many minds, was the victory of capitalism over all alternatives that defenders of the market no longer feel compelled to devise apologias for it as, say, social Darwinists did in an earlier generation. Capitalism is self-evidently the "natural" economic order, and by this logic, its moral rightness is also self-evident.

Yet a system is hardly moral when it allows a scant few to live in exquisite privilege and comfort by exploiting the labour of others. It is hardly moral if it requires those others, together with their spouses, to work ever longer hours for ever shrinking recompense. It is hardly moral if it demands that they labour for their livelihood, then fails to make work available— or makes it available primarily to those who are willing to perform it for inadequate wages. (Social ecologists would argue that the wage system itself, not to speak of the reduction of human beings to mere labourers, is immoral.) Further, a society is hardly moral if it makes nutrition, housing, and health care the privileges of wealth rather than the prerogatives of membership in the community. It is hardly moral if it reduces the aims of life to mere survival rather than encouraging individual sense and sensibility and the attainment of positive social freedom. Yet these immoral conditions are the sequelae of capitalism even in many of the wealthiest countries today, let alone the poorest.

The market existed, to be sure, in earlier periods of Western history, but in those days it was disparate and marginal, consisting of pockets of commerce scattered in the interstices of a society whose values and traditions were otherwise largely noneconomistic in any modern sense. Labour was exploited in precapitalist societies, to be sure; as we have seen, before the advent of more sophisticated productive technologies, toil not only existed but was usually backbreaking. Feudal and ecclesiastical tyrannies, too, could crush the human spirit.

Yet integral even to ancient and feudal lifeways was a base of village traditions and communal customs that were life-enhancing and that could provide individuals with a measure of emotional and physical sustenance. Even if people engaged in arduous labour, their work was not reduced to a commodity, or to a capacity that had merely exchange value; nor were their surroundings structured in terms of buying and selling. Rather, the market and its values were sequestered into limited areas of social life. Precapitalist mores of mutual aid and moral responsibility offered refuge from truck and barter and, where necessary, a degree of resistance to it. Even as recently as the mid-twentieth century, capitalism was still merely one component—albeit a basic one—of many social relations in Europe and North America; it was still possible to find a refuge from it in precapitalist social and political formations, including a community life that vitally sustained nonmarket pursuits and mores.

But today capitalism is permeating and colonizing even those once commerce-free domains of society. Today it is primarily for their participation in the capitalist system—that is, for their economic productivity and their purchasing power—that people are valued, rather than for their contributions to civilization, or for their public or community service, or even for their moral decency. Commodity relationships, competition, and the values of gain are infiltrating into every pore of society, into familial, educational, personal, and even spiritual relationships, resulting not merely in a capitalist economy but in a capitalist society. Where the commodity is so ubiquitous, capitalism might well be perceived as "natural."

It is not by accident, it should be understood, that com-modification is becoming so deep-seated, so ubiquitous. The capitalist system has expanded because it is organized around a law of "grow or die," an imperative of rivalry and expansion that compels businesses to compete in pursuit of ever greater profits. The commodification of ever more aspects of life, which today has reached extraordinary proportions, is merely one outcome of this competitive process. The market economy is interlocking economic life ever more tightly on a global basis, seeking cheap labour and friendly authoritarian governments willing to discipline the labour process, for the purpose of gen-erating ever more profits for the owners of capital. Far from restraining capitalist expansion, Nation-States facilitate its operations, doing its bidding and catering to its imperatives. Driven by this "grow or die" dynamic, capitalism is tearing apart both human societies and the natural world, turning peo-ple into wretched drudges and soil into sand, rendering the planet less and less hospitable to complex life-forms.

Cooperatives

Horrified by the rapacity of these developments, many left-lib-ertarian and ecologically concerned people today argue for breaking up the large corporations and replacing them with smaller, alternative economic units. Their aim is, understand-ably, to reduce the scale of economic life and to lessen the toll that predatory corporations take on people and on the environ-ment.

The type of alternative unit they advocate varies, but it is usually a collectively owned and operated enterprise of some sort. It may be a producers' cooperative or some other worker-controlled enterprise, such as the collectivized and self-man-aged enterprises advocated by anarcho-syndicalists. Or it may be a purchasers' cooperative, such as a food coop, as advocated by many environmentalists. But whatever specific form it takes, those who advance it do so with the intention of creating a cooperative alternative society, of restoring economic life to a human scale, putting it directly into the hands of the men and women who are vitally involved with it.

Unfortunately, the competitive marketplace makes it difficult for any such alternative economic units to remain alternatives for long. For a hundred and seventy-odd years now, ever since the first socialistic cooperatives were essayed in Europe, cooperative enterprises have in the end been obliged to conform to marketplace dictates, regardless of the intentions of their advocates and founders.

This conforming process has followed a fairly standard pattern. First, a cooperative becomes entangled in the web of exchanges and contracts typical of all enterprises. Then it finds that its strictly commercial rivals are offering the same goods it offers, but at lower prices. Like any enterprise, the cooperative finds that if it is to stay in business, it must compete by lowering its prices in order to win customers. One way to lower prices is to grow in size, in order to benefit from economies of scale. Thus, growth becomes necessary for the cooperative— that is, it too must "grow or die."

In short, even the most idealistically motivated cooperative finds that it must absorb or undersell its competitors or close down. Ultimately, if it is to survive, it will have to seek profits at the expense of humane values (although making outward professions of humane values can be an effective marketing strategy). Little by little, the imperatives of competition will refashion the cooperative into a capitalistic enterprise, albeit a collectively owned and managed one. This development took place even under revolutionary circumstances in Spain in 1936, when enterprises that had been taken over by syndicalist workers for idealistic purposes ended up competing with one another for raw materials and resources, leading to takeovers by union bureaucracies or the State.*

In this fashion even the best-intentioned cooperative experiments are, lamentably, driven into the acquisitive embrace of capitalism. Of those that have lasted more than two or three years, the great majority have simply metamorphosed, under the pressure of competition, into ordinary businesses, or else perished, casualties of market-driven competitive forces. What they decidedly have not done is become more democratic; least of all have they posed a threat to the capitalist system. Even the celebrated Mondragon cooperative experiment, in the Basque country of Spain, is coming into conformity with the imperatives of the market.

Despite their poor record as a force for social change, cooperatives still hold an appeal for many well-intentioned people, who continue to look to them as a viable alternative to capitalism. Although cooperation is unquestionably a necessary part of the solution, cooperatives by themselves are insufficient to challenge the capitalist system.

Public Ownership

Any privately owned economic unit, then, whether it is managed cooperatively or by executives, whether it is owned by workers or by shareholders, is not only susceptible to assimilation by the capitalist system but will definitely be assimilated eventually, whether its members like it or not. As long as capitalism exists, competition will always require the enterprises within it to look for lower costs (including the cost of labour), greater markets, and advantages over their rivals, in order to maximize their profits. They will tend ever more to value human beings by their levels of productivity and consumption rather than by any other criteria.

*This Spanish history is explained more fully by Murray Bookchin in the interview at the end of this book.

If we are to create an alternative, cooperative society, profit seeking must be restrained or, better, eliminated. Since economic units are incapable of restraining their own profit seeking from within, they must be subjected to restraint from without. Thus an alternative economic unit that is to avoid assimilation must exist in a social context that curtails its profit seeking externally. It must be embedded in a larger community that has the power to bridle not only to bridle a specific enterprise's pursuit of profit but to control economic life generally.

No social context in which capitalism is permitted to exist will ever successfully curtail profit seeking. The expansionist imperatives of capitalism will always try to overturn external controls, will always compete, will always press for expansion. The simple fact, in the last analysis, is that capitalism itself must be eliminated. The present system must be replaced with a system that has both the desire and the ability to curtail or eliminate profit seeking in favour of humanistic values, practices, and institutions.

Such a society must be one that "owns" the economic units itself. That is, it must be one in which socially significant property—the means of production—is placed under public control or, insofar as ownership still exists, public ownership.

The notion of public ownership is not popular today. Its recent history has been nothing if not dismal, most notably in the case of the former Soviet Union. But in that and similar instances in which property has been nationalized, "public ownership" is something of a misnomer. "Public ownership" through nationalization means ownership by the Nation-State. Although the phrase "public ownership" implies ownership by the people, State ownership is not public ownership because the State, as we have seen, is an elite structure set over the people; it is not the people itself. "Public ownership" in the sense of the nationalization of property does not give the people control over economic life; it merely reinforces State power with economic power.

The Soviet State, for example, took over the means of production and used it to enhance its power, but it left the hierarchical structures of authority intact. The greater part of the public had little or nothing to do with making decisions about their economic life. Calling such nationalization "public ownership" is as obfuscatory, indeed as fraudulent, as calling Statecraft "politics" or calling a bourgeois republic a "democracy." Real public ownership would be ownership by the people themselves, in their communities not by the State.

The Municipalization of the Economy

Libertarian municipalism advances a form of public ownership that is truly public. The political economy it proposes is one that is neither privately owned, nor broken up into small collectives, nor nationalized. Rather, it is one that is municipalized—placed under community "ownership" and control.

This *municipalization of the economy* means the "ownership" and management of the economy by the citizens of the community. Property—including both land and factories—would no longer be privately owned but would be put under the overall control of citizens in their assemblies. The citizens would become the collective "owners" of their community's economic resources and would formulate and approve economic policy for the community. It is they, and not bureaucrats or capitalists, who would make decisions about economic life.

Citizens would make those decisions regardless of their occupation or their workplace. Indeed, they would ultimately make decisions for the entire economic life of their community. Those who worked in a factory would participate in formulating policies not only for that factory but for all other factories—and for farms as well. They would participate in this decision-making not as workers, farmers, technicians, engineers, or professionals, but as citizens. The decisions they made would be guided by the needs of their community as a whole, not by those of a specific enterprise or occupation or trade; they would serve the best interests of the community.

It has long been understood, in the history of political thought, that neither democracy nor political freedom can exist in a society where there are vast inequalities of wealth and income. Aristotle knew, as did Thomas Jefferson, that popular rule could not be sustained where resources were distributed very unevenly. Without a rough economic egalitarianism, democracy of any sort would most likely be ephemeral, giving way sooner rather than later to oligarchy or despotism.

Jefferson foresaw that a general and pervasive equality of condition would be necessary if even the American republic were to endure. Not long after his death, however, the relative economic equality of his day had already begun to yield to concentrations of private economic power. Today the disparities of wealth and income in the United States are so wide that the future even of the "democratic" masquerade at the national level is cast in doubt, let alone the potential reality of democracy at the municipal level. Economic inequality threatens to render a mockery of the Athenian ideal of the politically sovereign citizen who can make a rational judgment in public affairs because he or she is materially free from need or clientage.

In a rational anarchist society, economic inequality would be eliminated by turning wealth, private property, and the means of production over to the municipality. Through the municipalization of the economy, the riches of the possessing classes would be expropriated by ordinary people and placed in the hands of the community, to be used for the benefit of all.

Economic life as such would be absorbed by the community and brought under the control of the political realm, which would absorb economic decision-making as part of public business, the responsibility of the assembly. Neither factory nor land could ever again become a separate, competitive unit with its own interests.

The assembly's decisions, it is to be hoped, would be guided by rational and ecological standards. Indeed, the economy would become a moral economy. Classical notions of limit and balance would replace the capitalist imperative to expand and compete in the pursuit of profit. The community would value people for their positive contributions to community life, not for their level of production and consumption. Acting through their assemblies, the citizens would consciously and deliberately prevent economic entities from obeying capitalist imperatives of profit seeking rather than ethical strictures of cooperation and sharing.

The assembly would make decisions not only about production but about the distribution of the material means of life, fulfilling the promise of post-scarcity. "From each according to ability and to each according to needs"—the demand of all nineteenth-century communist movements—would become a living practice, an institutionalized responsibility of the political realm. Everyone in the community would have access to the means of life, regardless the work he or she was capable of performing; the community would see that a rough economic equality, based on morally and rationally formulated criteria of needs, would exist among all its citizens.

Over the wider geographical range, economic life would be controlled by the confederation of municipalities. The wealth expropriated from the property-owning classes would be redistributed not only within a municipality but among all the municipalities in a region. At the confederal level individual municipalities would share resources with one another and make decisions about production and distribution. If one municipality tried to engross itself at the expense of others, its fellow confederates would have the right to prevent it. A thorough politicization of the economy would take place, extending the moral economy to a broad regional scale.

Chapter 13

Dual Power

The "feeling of empowerment" is a sensation that is much sought—after in many religious, psychotherapeutic, and sometimes even political groups today. After participating in a certain activity, members of a group may remark enthusiastically that it made them "feel empowered." Members of a spiritual group, for example, may say that they "feel empowered" after participating in a religious ritual. People in twelve-step groups come away from talking about their addictions "feeling empowered." Members of an affinity group may "feel empowered" after expressing their rage in a protest action of one kind or another. Even individuals who use spiritual self-help nostrums will "feel empowered" after chanting "affirmations" to themselves, or after lying down, closing their eyes, and daydreaming through exercises in "guided imagery."

Power, however, cannot be obtained through daydreaming, or through rituals, or even through direct actions whose purpose is limited merely to protest. One may gain a pleasant sensation from such exercises, or even an illusory "feeling" of empowerment, but one will gain no actual social or political power whatsoever.

Power is not merely a spiritual or psychological feeling. It is a solid and tangible social fact and must be understood as such; the force and violence exerted by Nation-States and by corporations are today precisely matters of institutional power, backed up by police, courts, and armies. To ignore power's factuality is to bid farewell to reality and drift into an ethereal or psychological nirvana.

121

Nor has Michel Foucault done a service for the remanent left of our time by casting power as an all-pervasive phenomenon that, by implication, is intrinsically evil and hence inimical to any sort of freedom. Such reasoning leads to the conclusion that a left-libertarian movement must strive to eliminate not merely the State and capitalism and hierarchy but power as such.

But power can never be eliminated. Some persons in some institution will always be in possession of power, whether it be a dictator in a fascist State, or free citizens in democratic assemblies. The acquisition of power—popular power—far from being inimical to freedom, is a precondition for freedom. Politics is the art of gaining and using power in order to create freedom, specifically, in the direct democracy of confederated municipal assemblies.

It is crucial for ordinary people to unite in order to regain collective social power, because power that is not held by ordinary people is given over to the State. By the same token, if people are to regain power, they must do so by taking it away from the State. No institutional vacuum is possible: power is invested in either one or the other. Today the broad mass of people in the world lack precisely what they need most to manage their affairs satisfactorily—power.

The most important fact about power, then, is not whether it exists but who has it. For a libertarian municipalist politics, this fact means that just as the Nation-State historically gained power at the expense of municipal independence and liberty, whatever power the new confederated municipalities gain for themselves will be gained at the expense of the Nation-State. That is, either the confederated municipalities will increase their own power by diminishing that of the Nation-State, or else the Nation-State will retain and increase its own power by diminishing that of the confederated municipalities.

Dual Power

Over the long term, as the movement for change grows, more and more municipalities will democratize themselves and form confederations. Eventually, at a certain point, when a considerable number of municipalities have been democratized and confederated, their shared power will constitute a threat to the State.

The existing power structure will hardly tolerate the existence of a confederation of democratized municipalities that has created a democratic politics, an empowered citizenry, and a municipalized economy. The State will move against the new democracy in defence of capitalism and its own power. The movement will be at the mercy of the State if it fails to create a civic guard to protect and defend the concrete popular power that it has come to embody. Indeed, if the movement is to be serious about opposing the State, it must work to divest the State of its most important attribute: its monopoly of armed force.

Despite the current popularity of militias among far-right groups in the United States, the right holds no exclusive title to the militia tradition. For a century and a half, the international socialist movement recognized the necessity of an armed people or a citizens' militia. Every socialist international since the first one demanded that a militia be substituted for the army and the police. The anarchist and syndicalist movements, too, once considered an armed people to be a *sine qua non* for a free society.

No consistently radical position today can surrender the demand for an armed people without in effect making it possible for the State to continue to exist. Libertarian municipalism, as part of the socialist and anarchist tradition, thus calls for the ultimate formation of a civic militia, or civic guard, to replace the police and military forces. This civic militia would be under the strict supervision of the citizens' assemblies. It would be a democratic institution in itself, with elected officers.

The larger and more numerous the municipal confederations become, the greater will be their latent power, and the greater will be their potentiality to constitute a counterpower to the Nation-State. As they realize this potentiality, tension will grow between themselves and the State. The citizens in the confederations must clearly recognize that this tension is desirable—indeed, that their confederated municipalities constitute a potential counterpower to the State. They must recognize that they are essentially reviving the long historical conflict between the municipality and the State, and that their confederation cannot live in harmony with it.

In fact, the confederation of municipalities may eventually gain enough power to constitute a *dual power*, one that could ultimately reclaim complete power for the people. If and when this point is reached, the social and political conditions will likely be unstable. Sooner rather than later, most likely in a confrontation, the issue of who will have the power—the municipal confederations or the State—will have to be resolved. That is, power will have to be shifted toward the people and their communities, or else it will remain with the State and the professional practitioners of Statecraft.

Ultimately, the confederations will likely attempt militantly to replace the State with their own structures. By this time, it is to be hoped that the libertarian municipalist movement will have institutionally "hollowed out" the State power itself, winning a majority of the people over to its new civic and confederal structures. If the State's authority can be delegitimated in the eyes of most people, then hopefully it can be eliminated with minimal difficulty.

In Paris in 1789, and in St. Petersburg in February 1917, State authority collapsed in the face of a revolutionary confrontation. So denuded of power were the seemingly all-powerful French and Russian monarchies that they merely crumbled when challenged by the revolutionary people. Crucially, in both cases, the armed forces—ordinary rank-and-file soldiers—went over to join the revolutionary movement. What happened in the past can happen again, especially when an effective, conscious, and inspired revolutionary movement is guiding the process to that end.

Fostering the Tension

During the period when the dual power is being forged, the tension between the confederations and the Nation-State must be neither obscured nor relaxed. On the contrary, the libertarian municipalist movement must foster that tension by making clear its opposition to the State, and it must heighten and exacerbate it where it can (without being adventuristic or precipitous, to be sure). Only this way can the municipal confederation become a counterpower rather than a parliamentary party or other State-oriented entity.

Despite the acute importance of preserving the confederation-State tension, however, some members of the movement may lose sight of the need to perpetuate their oppositional status. It is always to be expected that individuals or groups in the existing social order will attempt to compromise the movement or coopt it by offering key members a short-term reward, such as a remunerative office in the existing power structure, in return for reorienting the movement along Statist lines, thereby compromising it. Susceptible movement members may find the temptation too alluring to resist and may betray the movement.

Some may betray it out of personal self-interest, but others may do so inadvertently, out of a well-intentioned but misguided belief that their action will widen the movement's base. It is easy to anticipate how such thinking runs: Many Nation-States today, for example, contain within themselves a variety of intermediate governmental units—like provinces in

Canada, states in the United States, and Länder in Germany. Because these intermediate units retain various powers for themselves as against the Nation-State, some libertarian municipalist members may mistakenly think that they represent a kind of decentralized or local power in their own right, and that citizens already possess, in them, a degree of local control.

They may imagine that even though they are not popularly run, these intermediate units still represent a level of local and potentially decentralized government. They may argue, quite innocently, among their fellow members that the movement should run candidates not only for municipal office but for office at these intermediate levels as well. Such arguments may be persuasive—after all, candidates who are running for "higher" office can reach more people, especially through the mass media.

If the libertarian municipalist movement wishes to retain its identity as well as its integrity, however, it should avoid campaigns for such offices. Provinces, states, and Länder are not popular institutions; they are small Nation-States in their own right, organized around repressive Statist institutions, and they function primarily as channels for the power of the centralized State and for the administration of its policies. When the confederation of municipalities arises as a dual power, these units will oppose it and align themselves with the State.

All offices beyond the municipal level, therefore, are vehicles for the State, and campaigns to gain them would relax and obscure the very tension with the State that the movement is trying to foster. By blurring the distinction between the municipality and the State, such campaigns would render nonsensical the educational efforts of the movement and blunt its radical goals.

Campaigns for State Office

If history, from ancient times to the present, has demonstrated anything, it is the implacable fact that State power is corruptive: that an individual who takes State office is inexorably refashioned by that office into a creature of the State, regardless of his or her idealistic intentions.

In the late 1970s and early 1980s, the Green movements that emerged in various parts of the world were decentralistic in their expressed political orientation. In the flushed idealism of their new-found existence, they passionately voiced principles of local democracy and control. Many European Green parties gained initial popularity sufficient to suddenly propel some of their members into electoral office—not only to provincial or Land office but even to federal or national office. Soon many of these officeholders conveniently "forgot" their erstwhile decentralism in the pursuit of attractive "political" careers and privileges, while the parties themselves let go of their basic grassroots principles and tried to make coalitions with the conventional bourgeois parties.

At first, the most frequently voiced justification for these electoral campaigns was that they were merely educational in nature, that they served to raise public consciousness. The impression, if not the promise, given by their advocates was that if Greens were elected to office, they would use that office merely as a platform for educating the broader public about Green ideas, and would not allow themselves to be placed in the service of the State. Other members, less mindful of their former ideals, argued that once Green candidates gained office, they could help bring about decentralization from the top down, empowering smaller local units of government by devolving power from above.

Such justifications, as it turned out, merely gained individual Green candidates votes that endowed them with the prestige and income of office. As officeholders, they worked for Green-style legislation that would reform the State and mitigate the impact of capitalism on people and the environment, but they did not advance radical aims by one iota or educate the public into a radical outlook toward the State. On the contrary, as more of their members took State office, the parties and their programs became less radical, and Green representatives sought reforms that had the effect of making the State seem more humane and respectful of public needs.

Nor have Green parties been the only case of disappearing radicalism. Historically, few of even the most principled revolutionary leaders were able to resist the corruptive effects of State power. Most often, dedicated socialists, communists, and even anarchists lost their moral and political integrity when they attained power in State offices. So regularly and so predictably has this "reverse education" taken place that it seems inexorable. We may conclude that to accept State office is to be "educated" in the ways of Statecraft, not to educate the public in radical anti-Statist politics; that it serves to perpetuate State power, not to expand a popular democracy; and that it may even contribute to deploying the State's authority and power against the resurgent popular democracy that one originally professed to support.

Since the heyday of the Green movements in the 1980s, other "independent" political movements have called for "grassroots politics" in a plethora of freshly minted third parties. In the United States they include the Labour Party and the New Party, among others. In the course of building the libertarian municipalist movement, some members may think it desirable to join forces with these parties, as a way to gain allies and expand the influence of the movement.

But once they join these ostensibly independent but intrinsically reformist parties, libertarian municipalists will likely hear over and over again the same argument: If it is acceptable to run for local municipal office, it is acceptable to run for "higher" office as well; after all, a person's effectiveness in "higher" office could be proportionately greater than in a less powerful one. By joining with a reformist party to wage an electoral campaign for gubernatorial, congressional, and other office, they will hear, the movement can attract greater public attention to libertarian municipalist ideas.

Members of the movement will have to repeatedly remind one another that their movement is not an instrument for gaining State office, still less for cosmetically "improving" the State or giving it a "human face." Libertarian municipalism is, rather, an ongoing struggle whose purpose is to create radical and emancipatory civic institutions, not to appropriate existing oppressive ones. It must struggle against the State from the moment of its inception and at every moment of its existence. The very fight for municipal confederations, for the municipalization of property,and for a direct-democratic politics is directed toward the complete remaking of society, not toward gaining reformist victories. If the movement is to create the revolutionary Commune of communes, it must do so by working every day to create a direct-democratic dual power as a counterpower to the State.

Campaigns for Mayor

Should libertarian municipalists run candidates for mayor? Some sympathetic people have argued that mayoral candidacies would be inconsistent with the struggle to create popular assemblies. As an executive office, they contend, the mayoralty is structurally and morally equivalent to the office of governor and prime minister and president, albeit on a smaller scale. Libertarian municipalists, by this logic, might run candidates for the local "legislative" body, the city council, but not for mayor.

It is the municipality as a whole, however, and not merely its city council, that potentiality exists in tension with the State. The municipality has a qualitatively different history from the State. The crucial factor about a municipal office—be it a mayor, councillor, or selectperson—is its municipal context, just as the crucial factor about the presidency, prime ministership, congress, or parliament is its State context. Mayors usually come under closer public scrutiny than do state and provincial officials, and their powers are far more controlled.

To run a candidate for mayor on a libertarian municipalist program is therefore qualitatively different from running a candidate for provincial or state governor, let alone president. The movement may well run mayoral candidates. It should, however, be committed to transforming the mayoral office into that of a chairperson, as well as to transforming the city council into a confederal council of delegates from the municipality's neighbourhood assemblies.

Libertarian municipalism gains its integrity precisely from creating and sustaining the dialectical tension between the municipal confederation and the Nation-State. Its very "law of life" consists in its struggle against the State and its attempt to divest it of its power and efface it. Unless the tension between the confederated municipalities and the State is kept clear and uncompromising in practice, the movement will lose its radical identity and meaning. Rather than distort libertarian municipalism this way, people who wish to compromise its identity would be better advised to join a conventional party.

Chapter 14

A Rational Society

Manifestly, once the dual power is resolved and the confederated municipalities have overcome the forces arrayed against them, sovereign power in society will be in their hands. Citizens may then bring the potentiality of this sovereign political realm to fulfillment by transforming society along rational and ethical lines.

To the extent that human beings can collectively sculpt the society in which they live, their means for doing so lie neither in the social realm nor in the State but in the political realm. The social realm, as we have seen, is involved with matters of the family, with the private matters of the individual, and with the economic aspects of life, with production and distribution. Family and individual matters are too narrow in scope to have a great influence on the rest of society; and while matters of production and distribution have greater influence, it is still partial; factories and workplaces are simply not places where decisions about all of society can be made, and economic life easily breaks apart into separate sectoral or entrepreneurial interests. The State, for its part, is not a place where people collectively shape society; it is a place where an elite few wield power over a majority.

Thus, the means for collectively reshaping society lie the political realm itself, in the place where decisions about how society is to function are explicitly and consciously made by the community. If decision-making is actually to be collective, it must be directly democratic—that is, its political institutions must be those of libertarian municipalism, based on the presupposition that every normal adult is competent to engage in community self-management.

Once people have collectively taken the reins of the decision-making power, then, they may plan and decide what kind of society they want to be part of and leave for future generations to enjoy and improve. The kind of society that they choose to create will be theirs alone to decide democratically. It cannot be ordained by theorists of libertarian municipalism. But to a great extent, the continued existence of a direct-democratic political realm will depend on whether the citizens rebuild the social realm according to the same ethical values and practices that undergird their political realm. It will likely not survive if the choices they make about the rest of society contradict those values and practices.

Among these values would be mutuality—a sense of mutual identification among citizens—and complementarity, a sense of responsibility for one's fellow citizens and their families and of obligation for everyone's welfare. If solidarity and reason infuse civic life, they would have to be grounded in a mutuality, a humanism and cooperation, that pervaded the rest of the society as well.

An ethos of cooperation and solidarity would have many social consequences, not the least of which would be an abolition of hierarchy and domination—not only of the State but of institutionalized social stratifications based on gender, race, ethnicity, age, and other status distinctions, stratifications that obstruct mutuality by virtue of the inequality and domination they entail.

A Moral Economy

This ethos would also have to infuse economic life if the political realm is to survive. A society organized along mutualistic, nonhierarchical, and communal lines would be most rational if it chose to replace the capitalist market economy with a moral economy, one whose members were possessed of a high sense of mutual obligation. It would replace classes and private property with cooperation and solidarity. It would replace profit with a recognition of mutual welfare. It would replace selling with sharing. It would replace rivalry and an illusory independence with reciprocity and interdependence. By replacing a profit-oriented economic nexus with an ethical one, it would transform economics into culture.

What would economic production look like in such a society? Onerous forms of production that required arduous toil or that were mind-numbingly tedious would be performed not by people but by machines in factories. The products and technologies essential for a post-scarcity society would be manufactured in industrial plants: durable goods and medical equipment, textiles, means of communication and transportation, machine tools, electronics, and so on. The productive technologies in these factories would be enhanced, far more than they are now, by processes of automation and cybernation that would allow the machines themselves to perform work with a minimum of human labour. Machines would make machines, as they already do to a great extent, and would require human intervention mainly for design and repair. Specialists would design reasonably unobtrusive factories, whose machines, in the event of a breakdown, would be repaired by maintenance people. But very little, if any, manufacturing production would require toil or tedium, let alone significant labour.

It may seem jarring to speak of such industrialism in the same breath as values of complementarity and mutuality. But industrialism is at odds with cooperation only if one considers industrialism to be synonymous with capitalism and the exploitation of labour. The industrial plant in a libertarian municipalist society would be collectively owned by the people and cooperatively managed as part of a moral economy, not a capitalist economy; perhaps more important, the minimization of human labor would create the material preconditions for a society infused by mutuality and cooperation. Indeed, it is the very productivity of such factories that would make possible the prevalence of the mutualistic ethos of the rational society.

This point is crucial. Past revolutions have foundered on the fact that their eras lacked a sufficiency in the means of production to free people from toil and provide them not only with a reasonable level of comfort but with the free time they need to engage in community self-management. Over hundreds of years of revolutionary activity, the mass of people who tried to transform social life along rational lines have been driven back, in part, because their technological level could not support the new social relations that could emancipate them from hunger, long hours of work, and class rule. Today, however, that technological capacity exists; a rational anarchist society would take the next step and use that technological apparatus to insure that people have freedom, rather than to subject them to domination and exploitation. (Some labour, of course, will always be necessary for the maintenance of the society; by the mutualistic ethos that prevailed, such socially necessary labour would be divided equally among those capable of performing it. But because most of the work would be performed by machines, such labour would not require much time to perform.)

Factory production, of course, need not preclude the handcrafting of objects that enhance life, for those who derive satisfaction from such activities. Indeed, factory production of the basic components of a crafted product would leave crafts-people free to concentrate on its more artistic and expressive dimensions. Those who enjoy weaving fabrics, for example, could let machines perform the tedious work of turning fibres into threads; but they could weave on handlooms for their own enjoyment, to produce textiles for friends and community alike.

So too, people who enjoy the sensuous experience of gardening could grow their own food if they chose, and the aesthetic pleasures of small-scale farming activities are considerable. But many people might not choose to spend time growing their own food, preferring other activities; they would obtain their food from agricultural processes that were partly or perhaps fully industrialized. The bulk of agricultural production, in fact, would be mechanized, allowing the onerous drudgery of hard farm labour finally to recede into the distant past.

Not only would industrialized agriculture be desirable, it would be necessary if society were to support growing human populations. It is, frankly, a naive fantasy, shared by some radical environmentalists today, to think that society could return to digging sticks, foraging, and horse-drawn ploughs, except on an individual basis to satisfy strictly personal desires. Nor is industrial agriculture incompatible with organic methods. Food cultivated industrially could well be organic, and the machines used for it would be designed to have minimal negative effects on the soil and its ecology.

The same principle of choice—and it should be recalled that without choice, there is no freedom—could be applied to the production of all manner of material objects. In effect, a person' s vocation would be a moral calling or a personal preference, not an occupation that they were coerced or otherwise compelled to perform. Without physically exhausting and tedious labour consuming most of their time, people would be free to live more creative, expressive lives, and their choice of activities could reflect their wishes rather than the stringent demands of the realm of necessity.

If production based on reducing human labour is a precondition for a moral economy, equitable distribution would bring that economy to fulfillment. Distribution would be consistent with the humanistic and cooperative values of a libertarian municipalist polity if it were participatory, affording the irreducible minimum of the means of life to everyone in the community. It would offer all community members the material means that they need to fulfill their human potentialities and to conduct an aesthetically pleasing and ethical life.

Needless to say, economic inequality would be nonexistent; the only inequalities would be those resulting from strength, age, health, and individual aptitudes. But these inequalities, rather than being pretexts for domination, would be compensated for socially, so that those who needed more support would have ready access to it. Operating according to the principle "From each according to ability, to each according to need," distribution would cease to be a matter of economics at all.

Without the capitalist economy, whose grow-or-die imperative is the primary force behind the ecological crisis, citizens would be free to reconstruct their social world along ecological lines. Cities could be physically as well as institutionally decentralized; town and country could be integrated into a unified whole and the historic conflict between them effaced. Fossil fuels would doubtless be eliminated, replaced with clean, renewable sources of energy—even in factory production. The world of nonhuman nature would no longer be conceived as a realm of scarcity, as capitalism conceives it today—with too few resources that must be fought for tooth and claw—but as a domain of fecundity and evolutionary advance toward diversity and complexity.

That the citizens in a new polity will be willing to recreate their society according to these principles is not something that we can predict with certainty. The essence of democracy, after all, is that they will have a choice. But insofar as they wish to preserve their direct democracy, their choices will have to be guided by reason. If they were to choose to restore the command factory labour system, for example, when it is no longer necessary, it would be irrational. It would be irrational for them to choose to restore capitalism and once again unleash the profit motive to wreak havoc on society and on the biosphere. It would be irrational for them to transform municipal confederations into States. It would be irrational to exclude an ethnic or gender group from political participation. A liberatory and ecological anarchist society would be impossible without an ethos of mutuality and complementarity; but that ethos, in turn, is unthinkable without the exercise of reason to support its values and practices against all the unsavoury alternatives.

Chapter 15

Today's Agenda

Today capitalism is threatening to commodify ever more areas of social life, to penetrate ever further into the private recesses of our lives, and to efface personality, let alone individuality. Urbanization is threatening to devour the city and the countryside alike, leaving community an archaism. The State threatens to absorb the very notion of freedom itself, and this drive is undermining the biosphere at an appalling rate, with consequences that are potentially catastrophic for all complex life-forms.

At the same time, many of these same institutions are exerting a strong inertial pull on political and social life that militates against radical change and that enmeshes people in existing institutions. The mass media sedate or transfix people into accepting their own domination and exploitation, defusing their inclinations to become something more than docile consumers and passive, adaptive subjects of elite rule.

Against the wide array of social forces that oppose radical change, men and women today will need a compelling motivation to undertake the social and municipal revolution described in these pages and to create the society proposed by social ecology. What could induce them to work to recreate the political realm, democratize their municipalities, and confederate them as a dual power against the State?

Undoubtedly the most important of their many possible motivations is that a rational anarchist society would provide conditions for the greatest possible human social freedom. The growing unfreedom and inequality in the world today may well propel people to rise up in outrage against their exploitation, domination, and even enslavement (although the specific event that may induce them to do so is unforeseeable). The notion of being able to manage one's own affairs, in community with one's fellow citizens, has an enduring appeal, even and especially in an era of growing powerlessness and deracination.

Nor is it possible that the Nation-State and the capitalist system can survive indefinitely. Even as this system is widening the divisions between rich and poor around the world into a yawning chasm of inequality, it is also on a collision course with the biosphere. Capitalism's grow-or-die imperative, in particular, which seeks profit at the expense of all other considerations, stands radically at odds with the practical realities of interdependence and limit, both in social terms and in terms of the capacity of the planet to sustain life.

Capitalism and the global ecology simply cannot coexist indefinitely. In the next century global warming alone is expected to wreak havoc with the climate, causing rising sea levels, catastrophic weather extremes, epidemics of infectious diseases, and diminished arable land and hence agricultural capacity. At the very least, hunger and disease will soar, while States will become even more authoritarian to repress social unrest. Increasingly, the choice seems clear: Either people will establish an ecological society, or else the underpinnings of society will collapse. The recovery of politics and citizenship is thus not only a precondition for a free society; it may very well be a precondition for our survival as a species. In effect, the ecological question demands a fundamental reconstruction of society.

In recent years this looming crisis has given rise to an ecological politics. As we have seen, the Green parties that have been formed in many countries tried to achieve their ecological and social goals by making use of Statist institutions but after only a few years were reduced to conventional bourgeois parties, whose professional elites practice Statecraft and support the very forces that are producing the ecological crisis, albeit with a green veneer.

But the Greens are only the most recent movement that has tried to realize radical-left goals in the corridors of the Nation-State. They were preceded most notably by the European socialist parties, based in an idealistic and principled movement that, a few generations ago, upheld a vision of a socialist society. Tragically, as the socialist movement was transformed into an assortment of conventional Statist parties, its vision was eclipsed by the pragmatics of gaining, holding, and extending power in State offices. Now, despite their original emancipatory visions, the Social Democratic Party in Germany, the Labour Party in Britain, the New Democratic Party in Canada, and the Socialist Party in France exhibit only superficial differences with their capitalist counterparts.

A century of such defeats has dispiriting effects. Time wears expectations thin, as one disappointment follows another. Talk of a "new politics" becomes unconvincing, especially when people who might be receptive to the idea have been led by bitter experience to conclude that such efforts mean nothing more than the creation of another mainstream party. In despair, they may decide to work incrementally, in a movement to address a single issue.

Yet the history of the left has shown that strictly single-issue movements are limited as well. To be sure, they have significance for protesting particular injustices, but the results they yield are minimal in proportion to the growing social and ecological changes that are necessary. Above all, they do not provide a program for building the ongoing institutions that are necessary for the reconstruction of society. Nor have they consciously aimed to create a political arena in which democratic activities could become a permanent presence in everyday life.

The lessons of a century of leftist activity, then, point to the conclusion that neither parliamentarism nor single-issue movements can fundamentally change society; workers' control of factories, for its part, leads primarily to collectivized capitalist enterprise. What alternatives remain? Any political movement today that presents itself as a challenge to capitalism and the Nation-State must be structured institutionally around the restoration of power to municipalities—that is, to their democratization, radicalization, and confederation.

Critics of libertarian municipalism have argued that the obstacles that stand in its way are insurmountable, especially the large size of many cities today. But if one is guided by this logic, one must conclude that the very existence of a given social condition means that it is immutable. The large size of many cities today is indeed a problem, but the very technics that have produced these cities also make it possible to reduce them to a human scale and bring them into balance with the surrounding natural environment. Eliminating the obstacles that stand in the way of social change is part of the process. To assume that problems that exist today are unsolvable, merely by virtue of their existence, is to surrender to them. The mere fact of existence could be used to justify acceptance of the State and capitalism, in which case left-libertarians might as well give up trying to replace them and become social democrats or liberals.

Capitalism will not provide its opponents with the popular democratic institutions they need to struggle against it. It will fight to the end to preserve itself, its social relations, and its State institutions, however much it may allow, or even welcome, the efforts of reformers to "improve" it and render it palatable. If a revolutionary people are to gain emancipatory institutions, they must create them on their own initiative. If they have available vestigial institutions on which they can build—like town meetings and city councils—so much the better. If such institutions do not exist, then they must create them from whole cloth. The task is harder, but it still can be done. While emancipatory traditions are helpful, they alone should not determine whether a movement to create a rational society will exist. In any case, the initiative for social change lies with the movement.

Although libertarian municipalism may seem utopian, the steps it advances are actually quite concrete. So, too, are the social problems that compel us to act. Global ecological breakdown is a problem that affects everyone regardless of class, and the desire to preserve the biosphere is universal among most rational people. The need for community is abiding in the human spirit, welling up repeatedly over the centuries, especially in times of social crisis. As for the market economy, let us recall that it is only two centuries old; in the mixed economy that preceded it, acquisitive desires were culturally restrained and many alternatives existed to modern capitalism.

What men and women have created in past centuries can certainly be recovered and advanced by people today. If our ancestors, with their limited technological and communications resources, were able to effect massive social changes, men and women today can do the same. Indeed, the new means at our disposal give us immeasurable advantages that they lacked.

We also have the advantage that in many places democratic institutions do linger within the sinews of today's republican States. The commune lies hidden and distorted behind the city council; the section lies hidden and distorted in the neighbourhood and its community centres; the town meeting lies hidden and distorted in the township; and municipal confederations lie hidden and distorted in regional networks of towns and cities. By unearthing, renovating, and building upon these hidden institutions, where they exist, and building them where they do not, we can democratize the republic and expand the democracy to create the conditions for a degree of social freedom unprecedented in history.

Radicalizing the direct democracy would impart a political fulfilment to the institutions that the movement has created. Hence the slogan for this libertarian municipalist movement—"Democratize the republic! Radicalize the democracy!"

Given the rapidity of technological and scientific change, the suddenness of social upheavals, and the certainty that capitalism's inherent imperatives for growth must be finite, it is impossible to predict what social conditions and opportunities will exist even a generation from now. What is clear is that the demand for a rational society summons us to be rational beings—that is, to live up to our uniquely human potentialities—and construct the Commune of communes to fulfil our very humanity.

Interview with Murray Bookchin

Murray Bookchin was interviewed on November 12, 1996, in Burlington, Vermont, by Janet Biehl.

Q: Murray, one of your anarchist critics has taken your slogan "Democratize the republic and radicalize the democracy" and, in a sense, cut it in half. He accuses you of wanting only to democratize the republic, omitting that you also want to radicalize the democracy. Could you clarify the meaning of this slogan?

A: In most republican Nation-States today, the civic liberties that exist within towns and cities today are the result of hard-won struggles that were waged long ago by popular movements of one kind of another. Many cities, it's true, didn't enjoy civic liberties. But those that did so gained them primarily by struggles on the part of oppressed sectors of the population—against nobles who claimed the cities as part of their own States or who were trying to incorporate the cities into the States they were trying to establish. It's true that in many towns and cities the most educated and well-to-so sectors played a hegemonic role in winning these liberties. But even so, they were always afraid of the more oppressed sectors of the population, who they usually exploited.

These hard-won liberties have been diminished over time and circumscribed by the well-to-do. Yet they still remain, either in vestigial form or sedimented into the political culture of the present time.

A libertarian municipalist movement today has to do two things. The first thing is, it has to try to preserve these liberties. And second, it has to try to expand them, to use them as a springboard for claiming greater civic liberties and creating new civic liberties, which foster the participation of the population as a whole, particularly by the oppressed sectors of the population.

So when I say we have to democratize the republic, I mean we have to preserve those democratic features that were won by people in the past. At the same time we have to go beyond

145

that and try to radicalize them by enlarging them in opposition to the State and those features of the State that have invaded civic life. I don't have to be told that many aspects of city and town life today are controlled by the Nation-State or by intermediate bodies, such as provincial and state governments that function in the interests of the Nation-State. There are State features in every town or even village, let alone every city, in the world today.

But the point is that besides these very powerful State features in civic life, there are also democratic features, or vestigial democratic features, and these have to be enlarged and radicalized. And radicalizing them, I argue, is the only way in which a libertarian municipalist movement can develop as a dual power against the State.

So the slogan describes an ongoing struggle that would involve simultaneously preserving and radicalizing democratic features and civic liberties. These two processes are both part of one large process of trying, ultimately, to confront the State with a sufficiently massive public power that can ultimately overthrow it and replace it with a libertarian communist society.

Today's Harsh Social Realities

Q: I'd like to ask you next about some of the concrete obstacles that seem to stand in the way of this process. One is the problem of transnational capitalism. Of course, libertarian municipalism is trying to eliminate capitalism as well as the Nation-State. But many people believe that the ability of the Nation-State to exert a restraining influence on capital is in decline, especially with the phenomenon of globalization. If even the Nation-State, with all its enormous powers, is impotent against capitalism, how can municipalities or confederated municipalities ever hope to challenge it? Municipalities are small, and confederated municipalities may not be well enough united. Wilmington, Delaware, for example, is the headquarters of DuPont. Is it really feasible to think that Wilmington could ever municipalize that transnational corporation?

A: It wouldn't happen right away. All right, take Wilmington. Even though it's a DuPont town, that wouldn't prevent a libertarian municipalist movement from emerging there. If I were a resident of Wilmington, I'd try to develop and participate in a movement that would initially call for the municipalization of the land around Wilmington, and that would create as many different alternatives as can be created, irrespective of DuPont and its giant factories. As for those factories, yes, ultimately the movement would have to take over the economy from the bourgeoisie. But by the time that happened the municipalities would be confederated and face-to-face democracy would have made them very strong.

The "globalization" that we're talking about today isn't new. The export of capital was a central subject of discussion in Lenin's book on imperialism and in Rudolf Hilferding's works on the subject in the early part of this century. Lenin saw the export of capital as the key feature of capitalism in his time. What's happening today is that capitalism is doing what it has logically been expected to do according to Marxist economic theory—namely, export capital, move all over the globe, and ultimately industrialize the entire planet.

So the mobility of capital has always existed—and it's been shown statistically that a great deal of that mobility takes place within single countries rather than from country to country. But the notion that plants just pick up and leave an area and go anywhere in the world has been greatly exaggerated. In the United States some corporations move their plants from the rust belt to other parts of the world like Mexico, but more of them move to the southern part of the United States, where unions are also weak and labour cheap. Of course a textile factory in the Northeast may close down and go to Malaysia. But more likely it won't—it will go to another part of the U.S. and get tax breaks and other emoluments.

As for those that do go to Mexico or Malaysia—well, the movement I'm talking about is one that would extend beyond the borders of the United States. If capital is going to function in an international way, a libertarian municipalist movement will have to be international too. It was long known in past socialist movements—from the First International onward—that the working class had to function internationally. And during the time of the First International there were extraordinary examples of workers from different countries helping each other. Members of the International in Belgium prevented strikebreakers from going across the border to France to crush strikes by miners. English workers collected strike funds for workers in France, which led to a great deal of solidarity between the two. It surprises me today that so much of the left has lost its sense of international solidarity, apart from quasi-Maoist remnants. In short, a libertarian municipalist movement would have to be international, as would any radical movement today. And we need a vital international, one with solid roots on a local basis.

As for the decline of the Nation-State, I think that notion is largely specious. Nation-States are undergoing certain mutations—especially the United States, Germany, China, and possibly Japan. These countries are becoming dominant in the whole constellation of Nation-States. For example, Germany today is doing with considerable success what Wilhelm II in 1914 and Hitler in 1939 tried to do by force of arms, namely colonize large areas of Europe with the Deutschmark, with German capital and industry, but this time under the name of the European Union and partly in collaboration with France. One could say the same about the United States in North America—it's essentially completing its economic colonization of Canada and Mexico, and it has still other ambitions, as it has had for two centuries, going back to the Monroe Doctrine, of colonizing the whole Western Hemisphere. These are Nation-States we're talking about, not only transnational corporations. Key imperialist Nation-States, in other words, have found new ways of functioning imperialistically, namely through their industrial and financial might, not simply warfare.

Q: But isn't the purpose of NAFTA and GATT and the EU to strengthen the corporations, not the Nation-State? It would seem that, if anything, the U.S. government's power is being weakened by NAFTA—for example, undermining its ability to pass environmental laws. Aren't these "free trade" agreements that are part of "globalization" trying to eliminate State interventions in the activities of corporations so that capital can reap greater profits?

A: Yes, I agree with you completely that the interests of the corporations are being facilitated enormously. And I'm not sure that the Nation-States are sorry about the power of corporations to circumvent certain domestic laws. The bourgeois State has always been at the service of capital. Note well, just recently, that the Clinton administration has dropped the Delaney Clause, the law that kept carcinogens out of foods. I was raising concerns about pesticides in food forty years ago, when Congressman Delaney was holding his hearings, and now all that is being undone.

So it's a sad commentary that many self-styled leftists are now turning to the bourgeois Nation-State for redress from capital! The dumbing of the left has gone so far that someone like Chomsky, who professes to be an anarchist, wants to strengthen or at least support the centralized State against demands for its "devolution" to state governments, as though the centralized State could be used against the corporations, which it has always aided in the long run!

But the question that I'm concerned with is, what is happening to the essential powers of Nation-States regardless of various international agreements? To what extent do some dictate to others? Under the excuse of the so-called "war on drugs," the United States is actually sending its helicopters—its military might—into Mexico, to repress groups like the Zapatistas and others. It's enhancing the police powers of the Mexicans in repressing the peasantry. It used to be able to do things like that only surreptitiously, as when it subsidized the contras in Nicaragua. But now it can extend these powers openly. European countries, too, have more freedom to use their police powers to aid other countries in what are essentially counterrevolutionary measures.

So that while, admittedly, the U.S. is "compromising" its own environmental laws (which the State was forced to adopt reluctantly, by environmentalists), it is still helping American corporations exploit foreign labour at a much cheaper rate—which the corporations would have done anyway and the State has more domestic police powers that it didn't have before. Look at the so-called antiterrorism bill that the Clinton administration recently passed—it's allowing a lot more wiretapping, and it's even threatening habeas corpus—habeas corpus, of all things, an ancient right dating back to medieval England. So while greater power is being given to the corporations in NAFTA and so on, States are also enjoying greater internal powers, and more openly, than they had before.

Ultimately the State always tries to expand the markets for corporations. Nobody should doubt that. There's a great danger in the course of overstating the extent to which the corporations are granted powers—and the export of capital, the expansion of foreign markets. One can easily forget the enormous role that the State plays, and the enormous powers that the State accrues in the process of expanding the corporations' powers. The two interact with each other completely. It's high time we started speaking of all existing States as bourgeois States, not only Nation-States.

Q: How will confederated municipalities keep themselves from being put into the service of the corporations the way the State is?

A: Firstly, confederated municipalities can try to mobilize the people on a grassroots basis. They can try to constitute themselves into a movement—although such a movement does not exist so far. Secondly, confederated municipalities can try to pose alternatives, materially as well as politically, to capitalism. To the extent that such movements grow, they can try to mobilize public opinion to a degree that generally eludes the capacity of parties—especially at a time when there's so much cynicism about politics—to actively counteract the expansion of, say, DuPont abroad.

Whereas I see no alternative in forming a party like the Greens, who are running Ralph Nader for president. Despite his seeming radicalism, he wants to operate entirely within the existing system. For my part, I'm speaking of forming radically different alternatives to the present system. I'm speaking of establishing a separate political culture, modes of organizing, modes of transforming both politically and economically not only for Delaware but the entire United States or Canada or any other country, whereas those who are operating within the present social framework are only trying to moderate the State, to give it a "human face." They thereby make it more socially acceptable, I may add.

I'll add something else. If a seemingly radical party becomes corrupted by parliamentarism, which has historically been the case with every single party that I know of, then that very party, that very parliamentary party will endeavour to moderate the existing situation, will in point of fact make it easier for the most vicious elements in society to have their way.

There's no libertarian municipalist movement now, although there's a lot of talk these days about local democracy in all kinds of different circles. Yet such a movement is the only recourse we do have to the parliamentary path, which would certainly lead to overwhelming compromises that ultimately, in the long run, would abet the power of the corporations and State alike. Of course, we could also join hedonistic lifestyle anarchists by running naked in the woods—and do nothing but nourish our egos.

Q: Another problem for this approach today, or any approach, is the growth of large cities into megacities. You've made it clear that large cities can be decentralized, and you've advanced a distinction between institutional and physical decentralization. But today megacities—like Rio de Janeiro, Djakarta, Shanghai, Cairo—are growing to immense populations as peasants newly uprooted from the countryside for various reasons move into them. These megacities stand to grow still further in the coming years, to 15 or 20 million people. Can they be communalized in the ways you've been describing?

A: I would have to say that in such giant cities, one would have the greatest difficulty in creating a libertarian municipalist culture and movement. But that doesn't mean it would be impossible. People still have shared communal interests, in everything from sewage disposal to education, from air pollution to traffic, and so on. That wouldn't change. And they still would have a reason to try to alter the physical structure of their neighbourhoods. A common civic culture could still be developed.

A very important phenomenon is that when many urban belts reach a large size, they begin to recreate themselves into small cities. I have the strongest doubts that 20 million people could live in a megalopolis without recreating smaller urban centres and ultimately constituting themselves into a conglomeration of relatively smaller cities.

And this is actually happening now, although it's being ignored in many discussions of urbanism. In the U.S.—and I'm more knowledgeable about this country than I am about other parts of the world—American megacities that seem physically like the huge urban conglomerations that are now forming elsewhere are, in fact, wrinkling internally into smaller and smaller city centres. The suburb in the traditional sense, those bedroom communities that were monotonous tracts, homogeneous enclaves of middle-class mediocrity—many of those are becoming nucleated now and are increasingly turning into fairly self-contained cities in the sense of having their own downtowns and their own industrial as well as commercial areas. In places where for years there was nothing but residential tracts, a regrouping is taking place in which office buildings appear, institutional buildings, schools, government buildings, and even new kinds of industries. People no longer go to the old "city centre"—they now go to new "downtowns" that have been recreated out of their suburbs. So that what were originally bedroom communities are becoming relatively viable towns.

Q: But aren't these new smaller cities very often bastions of privilege? They're made up of people who have fled the poverty of the centre cities and in their own private cities, they buy their own police forces, their own school systems—the residents are rich enough to finance their own private community systems. And the residents put up gates around these privatized cities to keep out what they think of as "undesirable" people.

A: Of course many of the new cities are privileged ghettos. In fact, I predicted several decades ago, in my book *The Limits of the*

City, that there would be a tendency toward a kind of ghettoization, in which the rich would separate themselves from the poor. We cannot ignore the possibility that ghettoization could lead to a very reactionary development.

But we're still in a process of transition. We don't know where these nucleated cities will go in the long run. They're not all hiring their separate police forces or developing independent educational systems. They're not all privatized jurisdictions with walls around them. It's happening in a disturbing number of cases, but nucleation is far from taking place everywhere.

On the other hand, even these enclaves are opening up a degree of nucleation that could ultimately be used in a progressive sense. Our job is to examine what potentialities exist that, in the event of a social crisis, would lend themselves to a libertarian municipalist approach. What may be a privileged city today may one day feel the buffeting of the economy in such a way that it becomes a fairly rebellious city. A totally protected community, breached by economic, environmental, and cultural forces in the society, may turn into a radical city. The future of these cities is not foreclosed by the locked gates that separate them from less privileged areas.

Bluntly speaking, we will either have socialism or barbarism. There's no question that barbarism is possible—in fact, in many areas of life it's all too advanced. But there are still many areas of life where it has not advanced very far, if at all. Nor do I exclude the possibility of failure. But if there's any basis for hope, it's in a libertarian municipalist approach that recognizes transitions that may very well take place even in some of the most guarded of these nucleated areas.

Q: One more problem that a libertarian municipalist movement faces today is the mass media. Today the media are exerting a stifling effect on the human spirit, dragging it down to the lowest common denominator, producing a devolution in consciousness. They promote the consumer society, cajoling us in every possible way to shop for things we don't need. For people who are trying to form a political culture that values a commitment to the common good and not just to the maximization of individual pleasure and self-interest, how can we counteract this immense cultural pressure?

A: A libertarian municipalist movement would be working on an intimate personal level that's hopefully outside the boundaries of what the media can touch. One thing that should be understood is that to the extent that the media become increasingly concentrated, they are becoming forces of alienation, and today more and more people genuinely resent them—these remote institutions that seem to be governing their lives. While the media do have a great deal of power over public opinion, they are also disenchanting millions. In fact, many people are disgusted with the media.

The third party movement in the 1996 election year, however feeble, and the unprecedented abstention from voting are evidence that many people in the United States couldn't find in any existing Statist organizations a meaningful response to their problems. They were fed up with media displays, with media attempts to treat them like juveniles and debase them with glitz. One has only to look at the popular reaction to the party conventions for the Republicans and Democrats in 1996—even the media have declared that they will no longer cover conventions if they're going to be so patently organized for television. There's a growing sentiment against this concentrated media hurricane, and a libertarian municipalist movement can take advantage of the public's alienation.

In fact, a libertarian municipalist approach would be the only kind that could hope to counteract the concentrated power of the media, because it tries to reach people at their community level, and provide them with ways of counteracting and opposing the impact of the media, by working at the level of face-to-face interaction.

Q: Still another problem today is time. More and more ordinary people—the ones who stand to be most empowered by libertarian municipalism, as citizens against the elites—are working at two and even three jobs just to get by. They don't have enough time even to see their families. How can we call upon them to show up at a public meeting when they have to make all kinds of compromises with their time just to read their child a bedtime story?

A: If people want to become human beings instead of organisms that merely survive, I would suggest that they have to make some compromises. If people today are prepared to accept a way of life that requires them to work throughout all their waking hours in order to subsist, then I would say that I don't understand what drives them to continue, other than some animal instinct for survival. It has been one of the most challenging demands of Western philosophy, especially Hellenic philosophy, that people should strive to realize themselves as human beings. If they're not willing to do that, if they absolutely can't do that, then others who can do it will have to act for them in their own behalf for a while, without condescension, without demanding privileges for doing so. The injustices that force so many people to work long hours have to be corrected so that they can finally be free to come to assembly meetings.

I would like to think that in a rational society, advances in technology, such as automation, would all but abolish toil, but that lies in the future. At present, people must make a moral effort to be free, to find the time—difficult as it may be—to attend meetings and take control over their lives.

Identity and Universals

Q: You frequently invoke ancient Athens and colonial New England as historical precedents for direct democracy. Yet the ancient Athenians were extremely patriarchal and had slaves. So were the New England Puritans, who also hanged Quakers and enslaved Native people. Aren't these societies so tainted with sexism and racism, so exclusive to white males, that they really cannot be used as models for any free society today?

A: Despite the consistent criticism I have received on this point, I do not now and never have upheld either ancient Athens or colonial New England as a "model." None of the historical examples I cite here or anywhere else represents a "model" of libertarian municipalist ideas—not classical Athens, not the various medieval cities and city confederations—and not even the revolutionary Parisian sections and the New England town meetings. None, let me emphasize, represents an ideal image of what could or should be achieved in the future.

All were significantly tainted by major shortcomings—notably, class divisions and antagonisms and the exclusion of women and often the propertyless from public activity. The Athenian ecclesia didn't admit resident aliens—metics—even though some of them had been living in the city for several generations. They had a closed conception of citizenship. Sometimes people acted abusively and arrogantly in the ecclesia. Citizens were easily swayed by self-seeking orators and demagogues. And their societies were far from being post-scarcity societies. In the absence of freedom from toil, the most hardworking sectors of the population were too tired to go to the assembly.

So there's no model anywhere for a libertarian municipalist society. Above all, a libertarian municipalist society would be a
rational society—but many of the cultures that produced these
institutions weren't even rational. The Athenians overlaid their
assemblies with sacred business, so their agenda was divided
between the sacred and the secular.

And there were many other defects, even though they've
been underplayed quite recently by Cornelius Castoriadis, who
claims that slaves were primarily the property of a small, wealthy
elite. This isn't at all true, according to Hansen.[1] I'd be the last one
to regard these cities as models. The city I envision as truly rational, free, and ecological has yet to exist, and all my references to
historical cities are designed only to show remarkable institutions
that existed in the past that deserve our deepest consideration. I
cite them not for what they constituted at any given time, but for
what they innovated historically, and for the tradition that they
established that remains unfinished today, a tradition that with libertarian municipalism might well be brought to its rational com-
pletion.

Q: Some friends in other parts of the world have had problems
invoking the New England town meeting, because it belongs to
American culture rather than their own. Or they feel that the sectional assemblies are indigenous to France and therefore not relevant to their area. Even democracy seems alien to traditions in
many parts of the world—it's been European in its origins. How
can these "foreign" ideas be made relevant to people in other parts
of the world, or can they? Should they instead look to indigenous
traditions, even though they may not be as clearly democratic?

A: My concern with democratic institutions is not specific to the
cultures from which they stem. Thus, it's not because I'm a Greek
that I talk about the Athenian ecclesia. I'm not a Greek. I'm not a
Frenchman, either, still less a Parisian, yet I've repeatedly invoked
the value of studying the Parisian sections. Nor am I Spanish,
although I invoke the *comuneros*. And I'm not a New Englander by
background—I've lived here only for about a third of my life, most
of which was spent in New York City. But the town meeting is a
remarkable case of direct democracy. Should I ignore it because I
live in New England now?

During the 1960s, to be sure, I was deeply concerned
about working from specifically American traditions. But that
approach didn't come from any American chauvinism on my

part—although I've been accused of that. I was opposing "New Lefties" who were talking to the American people in terms of German Marxism, Russian Leninism or Stalinism, and Chinese Maoism. That's not to say that Marxism was or is irrelevant to the United States, not at all. But in their understandable opposition to American imperialism, they were really venerating Chinese and Vietnamese totalitarianism. Today, many of them would like to forget the mischief they caused, in view of recent—quite foreseeable—developments.

In invoking Athens, New England, the Parisian sections, I was trying to show that left-libertarians had good examples institutions of freedom right, in some cases on their very doorstep. They don't have to look overseas, not even to Southeast Asia, still less to China.

It was always the institutions themselves that were my primary focus, not a romanticization of the cities. What would be the point of invoking the Athenian ecclesia or the Parisian sections if I were an American chauvinist? Obviously I was concerned with the structure and the feasibility of these institutions, and only secondarily that they were part of traditions that were complementary to American thinking.

If human beings are potentially rational, as Aristotle said they were, it's the rationality of the institutions that should count, not the traditions. I would have no compunction whatever about going to places that have no democratic traditions, either ideological or institutional, and trying to convey the benefits of a genuinely democratic society. My job would be to function as a propagandist and an agitator, and to talk to people about the new, not necessarily the old, even counterposing the new with the old—trying to explain why, on solidly rational grounds, not traditional ones, they should discard an old system and adopt a new one. Such an endeavour would help offset the extent to which people's oppression has become deeply rooted even in their own thinking. I don't think I'm being patronizing or elitist. There are traditions that we would do very well to get rid of, like female "circumcision," if you please, or the veiling of women, or mythical interpretations of what are really social problems, accounts that obfuscate and mystify the power of existing elites.

Nor would I, as a Jew, find it either enriching or rewarding to go back to traditions from the Hebrew Scriptures, which are really fairly bloody. I could go through my own "traditions" and select some and discard others—but I don't embrace them or reject them just because they're part of my ethnic background. My point always remains that if people are potentially rational beings, they should try to live in a rational society, irrespective of their traditions. I'd like to think that humanity has had ten thousand years of education out of the primitivism and traditionalism and customs that ostensibly are our cultural roots, not that we're going to try to revive traditionalism for its own sake.

Q: Sometimes when people form libertarian municipalist groups, they call a meeting of a popular assembly in their neighbourhood, but not very many people show up. A visitor from Moscow recently told us of having this problem. It's pretty disheartening. What would you say to these people?

A: Treasure those who show up. Treasure them. Try to educate them. Remember that even in a libertarian municipalist society, assemblies will not necessarily be fully attended. Not even ancient Athens was based on universal participation. The ancient Athenians operated under very propitious conditions for democracy and had a democratic culture, but even they established a quorum of only 5,000 people, out of a potential citizen body of 30,000. That's only one-sixth of the people who were eligible to attend. In other words, they were satisfied to get one out of every six citizens to come to the ecclesia.

And the most revolutionary sections of Paris were a marvellous flare-up of energy, but they too accounted for a minority even of the sectional population. They were often attended by only fifteen or twenty people out of one or two thousand. And usually it was only in times of crisis that more than a score or so people came to a given sectional assembly meeting, out of all those that could legitimately attend. Attendance at sectional assemblies varied very much according to what issue was on the agenda.

People may decide to attend or not to attend an assembly meeting, depending on their personal concerns, private concerns, degrees of interest, amount of free time, the agenda, their own level of social and political development, illness, who knows what. One sophist I know from New Orleans—John Clark—wants to claim that unless everybody attends an assembly, it is not truly democratic. He looks at the total population of a large city today, figures out how many people live in each neighbourhood, and comes to the conclusion that huge numbers of people would be allotted to each assembly—say, five thousand or ten thousand. And they would all have to come, it would seem, for this to be real democracy—but look, he says, there are too many of them for democracy. So libertarian municipalism is impossible—that's his argument. It's as if he puts a grid on a city of eight million and calculates how many people would have to come to the assembly in each little square.

But the assumption here is that every infant, every child, every Alzheimer's patient will have to attend if what we have is to qualify as a popular assembly. This becomes a logistical sophism that is meant to obfuscate rather than clarify. The most important thing about popular assemblies in a libertarian municipalist society, one that has in time been decentralized physically as well as institutionally—and I don't mean scattered farms all over vast prairies—when all of this has been finally achieved, it would be a miracle if out of all those who are even physically capable of coming to an assembly, even a majority, would do so.

What counts is that the freedom to attend exists. This freedom stands as a sentinel over any authoritarian or hierarchical tendencies. The doors are open, and indeed it would be outrageous if people were forced to attend. Such an endeavour would be not only unrealistic but a travesty of human freedom—namely, the right not to attend as well as the right to attend. The main point I wish to make is that the popular assemblies would be open to everyone who lives in a municipality and is of a certain age, without restriction, and that people would be encouraged to attend and would be informed about the topics that will be discussed, so that they could decide if they want to engage in the act of democratizing. I would be surprised indeed if everyone in a community who was able to attend did attend, even a meeting where the most important decisions were made.

Another important point: Libertarian municipalism isn't exclusively a movement to create popular assemblies. It's also a process of creating a political culture. In most places a libertarian municipalist movement wouldn't be successful for years—I can't say how many—in convincing people that it offers a solution to the present political and economic impasse. Libertarian municipalism is a process, and it's a movement that tries to develop this process, to enlarge it, to win people's minds, even before libertarian municipalist institutions are established. The battle will have to go on, certainly past the remaining years of my life.

So one shouldn't confuse a libertarian municipalist movement with a libertarian municipalist society, although obviously the goal of the movement is to create the society. Nor should one confuse the process of education with immediate success here and now.

I will make a prediction, though: Were libertarian municipalists to succeed in establishing popular assemblies, in whatever
form, in certain communities, the founders of the assembly themselves would be in a minority, because an attempt will be made by
other interests, including class interests, to take over the assemblies. History has to be on our side. Many misjudgments will be
made, many failures will occur, many retreats will be necessary,
and years will pass when there will seem to be no positive
response to the propaganda of such a movement. But what's new
about that? It took the anarchist movement some seventy years to
take root in Spain. It took Russian revolutionaries almost a century of work to alter consciousness enough and to finally shake up
the Russian people enough to the point where they were ready for
the demolition of the czarist autocracy.

One problem I have today is that people want immediate
or quick results—it's one of the major diseases of the boomer generation. The 1960s upsurge, with all its generous ideals, fell apart
partly because young radicals demanded immediate gratification
and sensational successes. If people today think that politics
should be like a vending machine, where you put in your quarter
and out comes a candy bar—if that's what they think, then I would
recommend that they go back into private life. People have to be
prepared, to be steeled, to have the character—they themselves
have to embody the political culture of the future in their character to create a movement that might someday change society so
that it is libertarian, communalist, and political in the best sense of
the word.

The Nature of the Movement

Q: You've criticized alternative economic efforts, like cooperatives, saying that in the end they fit well into a capitalist society. Yet
your municipalized economy would certainly be organized along
some type of cooperative, as opposed to competitive, lines.
Alternative economic forms would very likely be needed there—
for example, municipally owned cooperatives. When you criticize
cooperatives, are you saying that efforts to build them are entirely
irrelevant to a libertarian municipalist movement?

A: No, I don't oppose cooperatives in principle. They're invaluable, especially as schools for teaching people how to cooperate.
I've only tried to show that we're not going to be able to eliminate
capitalism by colonizing it with ever more cooperatives, since

cooperatives are going to function like capitalist enterprises in many respects—that is to say, they'll become part of the market system, whatever the intentions of their founders.

Back in the 1840s Proudhon had the idea—and he wasn't the only one—that by creating cooperative peoples' banks and other kinds of cooperatives, capitalism could be replaced by them. Today, if I were to follow Proudhon, I would have to think that many small credit institutions could eventually replace Chase Manhattan, that small cooperative grocery stores could eventually replace supermarket chains. I would have to believe that small chemical factories could replace the DuPont corporation in Delaware.

The value of cooperatives today is that they teach people how to cooperate. But generally what happens in most cooperatives, in my own personal experience and in historical experience, is that they become bourgeois enterprises in their own right, getting into the competitive situation that the market produces. Those that don't, disappear.

Now "municipally owned cooperatives" would not be cooperatives in the conventional sense of the term. These would not be single private cooperatives or federations of private cooperatives. They would be "owned" by a community, meeting in popular assemblies. So they would operate as part of the community, not on their own, and they would be answerable to the community. Not only would these distinctly social cooperatives be "owned" by the community, but many of their policies would be decided by the community in assembly. Only the practical administration of these policies would fall within the purview of the individual cooperative.

But not only would the community as a whole determine their policies, the general public would establish a kind of ethical relationship with the cooperative, by virtue of the fact that the cooperative is integrally part of the public. This is one area where a political culture goes beyond the strictly institutional politics of the assembly and confederation. Not only would the economy be municipalized; but the political culture would help create a moral economy in the community, a new type of economic relationship between citizens and the sources of their subsistence, whether they be producers or retailers.

Under those circumstances of municipalization and a political culture, there would be no danger of each cooperative being a free-floating enterprise in a capitalist market. We would no longer have an authentic market in the bourgeois sense. In the

bourgeois market the buyer-seller relationship is not only competitive but anonymous. Municipally owned cooperatives could very
well subvert the market, because the community would own them
and because citizens would have an ethical responsibility toward
perpetuating them.

I don't believe the bourgeoisie would tolerate this development in the long run. Libertarian municipalism will not creep up
on capitalism and pull the rug from underneath it suddenly.
Everything I'm describing involves a confrontation, sooner or later,
not only with the State but with capitalism. Libertarian municipalism is meant to awaken a revolutionary development in the communities that in varying degrees follows libertarian municipalist
practices.

How this development and confrontation will occur is
impossible to foresee. Suffice it to say that they can open a wide
door for the improvisation of "strategies" that no speculation on
my part can possibly predict. Where such a confrontation would
lead, how it would unfold, I don't know, but I do know that if libertarian municipalism were embraced by a sizable number of communities, we would potentially, at least, create something like a
revolutionary situation.

Q: Some libertarian socialists have argued that you are too quick
to rule out workers' control. "Worker," they argue, is hardly a particularistic category anymore. Most able-bodied adults of both
sexes today are workers. Since the category is so general, why
can't a libertarian municipalism be combined with workers' control?

A: Yes, the great majority of people have to work in order to earn
a livelihood, and a sizable proportion of them are productive workers. A huge number of workers are unproductive as well. They
operate entirely with the circumstances and framework created by
the capitalist system, such as shuffling invoices, contracts, credit
slips, insurance policies, and so forth. Probably nine out of ten
"workers" wouldn't have any work to do in a rational society—one
that would not require insurance or any other commercial trans-
actions.

In a libertarian municipalist society, the assembly would
decide the policies of the entire economy. Workers would shed
their unique vocational identity and interests, as least as far as the
public realm is concerned, and see themselves as citizens in their
community. The municipality, through the assembly of citizens,

would control and make the broad decisions for its shops, lay down the policies that they should follow, always working with a civic outlook rather than an occupational one.

The supposition made by people who want to include workers' control in libertarian municipalism is that once we've democratized the society as a whole through the popular assembly, we would want to democratize the workplace itself and give it over to the workers to control. Now, what would that mean? Well, unless the workers in an enterprise really begin to see themselves primarily as citizens rather than workers, then we're opening up the very strong possibility that they will claim authority over their workplaces at the expense of the popular assembly. To the extent that you withdraw power from the popular assembly and give it to the workplace, to that extent you open cracks in the unity of the popular assembly and increase the possibility that the workplace itself will act as a subversive element in relation to the popular assembly.

Let me put it simply: The more power the workplace has, the less power the popular assembly has—and the less power the workplace has, the more power the popular assembly has. If workers' control is to become a major emphasis of our program, we will be diminishing the power of the popular assembly and thereby opening the possibility that the workplace will accrue power at the expense of the popular assembly.

And as I've said, the mere takeover of a shop and the operation of that shop by the workers does not remove the probability that they will develop—indeed, enlarge—an ever-present sense of a special entrepreneurial interest. Workers' control can easily result in workers becoming particularized, whatever their jobs may be. In anarcho-syndicalist Barcelona in 1936, workers who had taken over, say, a textile factory often pitted themselves against their own comrades in the same industry who had also taken over a similar shop. That is, such workers often became collective capitalists, as Gaston Leval pointed out in his account of Spanish collectivization in the cities,[2] and they competed with each other for access to raw materials and markets. All of this occurred even though the workers professed to be anarcho-syndicalists working in the same industry, under the same black and red flag, and belonging to the same syndicalist union! As a result, the union had to reregulate the industries in order to prevent these collective capitalist practices. Ironically, the CNT bureaucracy took control of the shops and essentially diminished the workers' control in order to maintain some kind of cooperative approach.

If shops are permitted to formulate the policies governing their behaviour without regard for the community as a whole, then such shops may very well follow paths that are not only divergent from those of the rest of the community but also in conflict with it.

Hopefully most trades will one day be mechanized—especially the more onerous and routine work operations. And by the way, that is not a completely utopian idea. Ultimately I believe that so much work will be taken over by machinery that the problem of workers' control will be virtually meaningless, and the whole issue will dwindle to the point of insignificance. I stand in flat opposition, on this score, to self-styled anarchist primitivists, such as the *Fifth Estate* mafia, who profess to oppose any advances in technology under all conditions.

Q: What is the relationship of a libertarian municipalist movement to direct action?

A: Libertarian municipalism is the highest form of direct action. It is the direct—indeed, face-to-face—self-administration of a community. People act directly on society and directly shape their own destinies. There's no higher form of direct action than self-determination.

Having said that, I believe emphatically that it's part of every radical political education to engage in direct action by trying to stop, say, the building of a development or some abusive, economically aggressive, vicious enterprise, indeed by taking social and political actions in every issue that arises today. These could involve sit-ins—the American labour movement in the 1930s was built on the occupation of factories by workers, after all. Not only is a strike a form of direct action, so is the occupation of a factory—in fact, it's an even more radical form of direct action that involves a transgression of the laws that protect the private property of the bourgeoisie.

To what extent these actions can lead to violence, I don't know. But I don't believe, either, that the bourgeoisie will surrender its status, still less its holdings in society, voluntarily.

Q: Will a libertarian municipalist movement have leaders?

A: There will be leaders everywhere, wherever there is a struggle. Does the existence of leaders necessarily mean the existence of hierarchy? Absolutely not! The word *leader* shouldn't frighten us away from recognizing that some individuals have more experience, maturity, character development, and the like, than others. These distinctions definitely exist, they're very real. To dismiss them and say that everyone is at the same level of knowledge, experience, and insight is a preposterous myth that is subverted by all the realities of everyday life. And not only the realities of everyday life, but also biological reality. People who have lived longer can often be expected to know more than those who are very young. Not even a precocious twelve-year-old could have the wisdom of someone who's lived three times his or her life and had a wealth of experiences. Biology renders it impossible for a child to have the knowledge of an adolescent, for an adolescent to have the knowledge of an adult person, and so on.

That doesn't mean that the more knowledgeable people will use their knowledge to dominate others. A leader is as much an educator as any person who offers people a sense of direction. In fact, we desperately need people to educate us. I have a great deal of trouble with anarchists who reject leadership altogether. There's no more subtle tyranny than the "tyranny of structurelessness"—which can also involve the tyranny of a false interpretation of equality—namely, that we all know the same. There's a big difference between saying that we all already know the same and saying that we are all capable, potentially, of learning and sharing knowledge on a potentially egalitarian basis.

Which raises the question that Hegel did once, in his early theological writings, about the difference between Socrates and Jesus. Socrates was an indubitably a leader, and he was loved as a leader—but as one who tried to overcome the difference, through education and dialogue, between what he knew and what the young Athenians around him knew, thereby trying to create a level playing field of discourse. Many of his dialogues consisted of overcoming the difference. Jesus, on the other hand, was a leader in an authoritarian sense. He made pronouncements that no one in his presence could possibly contradict without fearing his wrath. It's quite different to try to enforce obedience to the Ten Commandments because God supposedly ordained us to do so, and to explore them and find out what is valid and what isn't, to provide natural rather than supernatural reasons for obeying any idea. Parts of the decalogue are very regressive, such as Yahweh's injunction that he is a jealous god who will tolerate no other gods—and by inference, no contradiction.

Be that as it may, a leader does not make an elite, nor does he or she necessarily become an elite. Leadership as such is not necessarily hierarchical. A leader may simply be someone who knows more than others about a particular kind of situation and thereby plays a leading role in advising people on what they should do to address it. He or she doesn't dominate people or demand their submission. In a rational society, of course, leaders would not have the power to force people to do what they didn't want to do. Their sole source of influence is persuasion. And above all, they would be accountable to the rest of the people—that is, their actions would be under constant scrutiny.

Nor do I regard vanguard organizations as necessarily authoritarian. Ironically, more than one anarchist newspaper in the past has been named Vanguard, and more than one anarchist work has called for the formation of a vanguard organization. *Vanguard* organizations can give a movement a sense of direction, a map of how to go from here to there—and help mobilize them in systematic actions to change society.

It's tragic that the words *vanguard* and *leader* were discredited by the 1960s "New Left," because of the experiences of Stalinism and Leninism. In many revolutions there were immensely important, even decisive leaders and organizations that carried the revolutions forward, and in the absence of such decisive figures, the revolutions collapsed. During the Paris Commune Adolphe Thiers, who led the counterrevolution against the communards, was holding the revolutionary Auguste Blanqui as a prisoner. The Commune wanted Blanqui back, and they tried very hard to gain him in exchange for their own hostages, even the archbishop of Paris. Thiers shrewdly knew that giving the communards Blanqui would be equivalent to giving them a full division of troops, because Blanqui would have insisted on marching on Versailles and checkmated the counterrevolution. So one can't just erase the important role that many individual and organizational leaders have in history, even though there is always the danger, in a revolution that manages to make any degree of headway, that a leader can turn into a tyrant, and that an organization can turn into an elite. There is no substitute, in dealing with this danger, for intelligence and countervailing institutions that prevent leaders and organizations from becoming tyrants or elites—certainly not opposition to leaders and organizations as such.

Q: You've distinguished in the past between intellectuals and intelligentsia. Intellectuals are those who are endemic to the academy, while intelligentsia are the educated, theoretically minded individuals who are part of the public political culture that accompanies a revolution. Do you see an intelligentsia as playing a role in a libertarian municipalist struggle?

A: An intelligentsia is indispensable—and here I differ with all those academic intellectuals who denigrate the importance of an intelligentsia. It's amusing that professors, ensconced in the university system, would denounce an intelligentsia as an elite. I think it would be wonderful if everyone were a member of the intelligentsia, in a living public intellectual life, where ideas are part of the everyday milieu—indeed, where philosophy, ethics, and politics are not simply subjects of study but are lived practices.

For me, it is inconceivable, notwithstanding injunctions from various anarchist theorists, that the garnered wisdom of a true member of the intelligentsia can be ignored. I made a close study of revolutions while I was writing *The Third Revolution*, ranging from the Peasant Wars of the 1520s in Germany clear through to the Spanish Revolution of 1936. So closely did I study them that I felt as if I were brought into the very streets of these revolutions. This study made it immensely clear to me that these revolutions could not have hoped to succeed or even advance very far, without the knowledge—and even the leadership, in the best of cases—that intelligentsia or public intellectuals provided. What would the French Revolution have been without Jean Varlet, who stood head and shoulders above the best of the Jacobin leaders? What would the American Revolution have been without Thomas Paine? What would the revolutions of 1848 in Paris have been without a man of the calibre of Blanqui to inspire them? What would the Paris Commune have been without Eugène Varlin? What would the Russian Revolution have been without Martov, who foresaw the dangers of a Bolshevik autocracy? It's essential that we recover this waning tradition of thinkers who live a vital public life and at the same time are part of a lived revolutionary social and political environment.

Q: When a libertarian municipalist movement runs candidates for office, it will need an electoral program. What kinds of things should be on this program? If we put only our short-term goals on the program, we seem like only a reformist party. But if we only put in our long-term goals, like abolishing capitalism—well, many people aren't ready to hear that yet. Should we wait till ordinary citizens are somehow educated in these ideas before we run a libertarian municipalist campaign? Or should we run the campaign in order to educate people? How should we strike the balance between long-term and short-term goals?

A: The short-term goals in a program are designed to attract people eventually to support the movement's long-term goals. People might well support a libertarian municipalist candidate because they agree with the short-term goals on the program, and at first they may or may not agree with the long-term goals. I'm sure that after the Second World War millions of people in Britain who were afraid of socialism still voted for the Labour Party, even though the party expressed a long-term commitment to a form of socialism. Many very pragmatic problems would have induced them to vote for Labour, and they also had a vague aspiration that "a better world," which was designated by the word *socialism*, should come out of the war. Hence the enormous victory of the Labour Party toward the close of and after the war.

A libertarian municipalist movement would, of course, fight for the redress of specific injustices, and these should be in its program, even as it fights for the broader goals of freedom and direct democracy. But fighting against injustices alone, without offering an ideal of freedom, will not get to the root of the injustices that we want to correct. One anarchist I know has recently said that he still has a "vision" of an anarchist society, but that it's somewhere off in the distance. At present he works to fulfil his more short-term "goals," goals that involve correcting injustices—including the strengthening of the State, no less!

But the struggle against injustices can't be separated from the struggle for freedom. If it is, we'll still be burdened by the same social order, slightly or perhaps significantly more just, but still one that inevitably must inflict increasing damage on society and the natural world. A living connection must exist between our vision and our goals, such that our visions feed into our goals and give them immediacy. Otherwise, if goals and visions are bifurcated, we're functioning more as caretakers of capitalism, who are giving it a human face, rather than as revolutionaries trying to overthrow the root causes of all these injustices, as well as restrictions on the freedom and self-realization of all human beings.

So a libertarian municipalist program wouldn't make short-term demands without also making long-term demands at the same time. In the Left of the 1930s and 1940s, we used to call these the minimum and maximum programs. But the relationship of the minimum program to the maximum program can best be elucidated through the transitional program, a useful term invented, to the best of my knowledge, by Trotsky. A transitional program is meant to link the small steps that can be taken immediately with the ultimate goals, like communism or socialism.

For a libertarian municipalist movement, the transitional program might link a specific demand, like stopping "growth," to the long-term, maximum demand of replacing capitalism with a moral economy. And it would certainly link a simple, immediate demand like "better local administration" with the movement's long-term goal of direct democracy, calling for changes in a city charter that would allow for public assemblies and then demanding that these public assemblies be endowed with increasing powers.

As the libertarian municipalist movement gets underway, direct action might well be used to advance these demands and bring them to public attention. But first the movement would call for public assemblies here and now, and the establishment of civic centres where these assemblies could convene. Let us say these assemblies are formed, on an informal basis, and hopefully become a forum for neighborhood discussions. It may happen at first only in certain portions of a city, but those neighbourhoods may then become examples for parts of the city that are not, as yet, in political motion. Soon people, generally, will begin to see that something is going on in their own city, and they might start to do the same thing.

Increasingly, the assemblies may pass resolutions raising a variety of demands—anything from greater control over city services, to more fire stations, to improved and more numerous schools. The movement begins to campaign around these resolutions, presenting them as popular demands. The citizens speak, as it were. But most important, the movement raises the demand for changing the city charter so that the citizen assemblies have ever more, if not complete, legislative power.

In any community the people involved in the libertarian municipalist movement are likely to be a small minority within the very public assembly they have inspired. Other citizens in the assembly will probably still be fairly cautious and conservative. It is the job of libertarian municipalists to debate with these citizens over various issues in the assembly, to counter their objections, and to explain the broader social and political forces at work in society. In the process they try to educate everyone else. Let us suppose that real estate interests go to an assembly meeting in order to sell the community on a particular development or housing project or office complex. Or a manufacturer shows up and holds out alluring promises of more jobs if the community allows him to build a factory there. The libertarian municipalists have to try to stop them by demonstrating in detail the dangers that these proposals pose for their fellow citizens—and in the process, hopefully, they will educate them.

Many people, I have to say, have a difficult time seeing libertarian municipalism as process. But I contend that that is exactly what we are dealing with. Libertarian municipalists begin by making everyday demands for justice on specific issues, demands that challenge various capitalist interests such as real estate, construction, and retail interests, and the like. The movement then expands and expands—at the same time that it demands, through popular assemblies, more and more power from the state or the province and the Nation-State for the assemblies. This is a dynamic process that involves an ever greater enlargement of potentially democratic institutions—which, incidentally, no bourgeoisie has ever wanted to give to the people—calling for a charter if there isn't one, or a revision of the charter if there is one. These are all potentially very confrontational issues for grassroots power. The libertarian municipalist movement plays a major role in this process. Without a movement I doubt if the development I've described could continue to its logical conclusion.

Then if these developments have occurred throughout a particular region, confederations could begin to be formed. Throughout the process, the movement would be forming a dual power. The transitions would involve confrontations of various kinds all along the way, including direct action, and all of them would be enlarging the democracy within the republic, while continually radicalizing the democracy. Finally we would be confronted with a revolutionary situation, where a direct challenge could be presented against the State.

Because ultimately, as this political culture expands and grows, gaining the support of an ever greater number of people, it would have to end in its final "vision" if the movement presses forward in a dialectical manner to its maximum demands. It would confront the State power in a significant way. It could hardly "sneak up on" capitalism, or subvert the State from below, or make a gradual transition. It would have to confront capitalism and the State at every step along the way and push them back as far as possible until the confrontation acquires revolutionary proportions. From there on the lived development itself would decide which approaches, measures, or (to use a word I don't like) "tactics" the movement should adopt.

I am not describing an easy process. But if it is utopian to fight for the municipalization of the economy and the formation of libertarian confederated municipalities, what alternative do we have today? To build a political party that—judging from the histories of the German Greens, the British Labour Party, and third parties in the United States—is certain to degenerate into part of the State apparatus or simply disappear? What alternative is there to libertarian municipalism? How else are we going to square the demand for the "Commune of communes"—the traditional libertarian slogan of socialists, anarchists, and communists—with our politics? By falling back on our private experiences, going into Taoist meditations, or engaging in sensitivity sessions and encounter groups, as so many lifestyle anarchists desire?

What alternative is there? To work with the myth that we can eat away at the capitalist economy by starting cooperatives? In the 1840s and 1850s, Proudhon had a certain basis for thinking this could work, especially in France, before capitalism was very developed, while every grocery store was still a family store, not a supermarket chain. When industry and retailing were still small. But not today. Or are we going to call for the nationalization of the economy? But if we do, we'll only end up reinforcing the State power with economic power. Or maybe we'll call for market socialism—in my opinion, an oxymoron, as though the market didn't generate its own internal forces that lead to capital concentration.

The alternatives are private property, nationalization of property, or municipalization of property. I leave it up to anyone who has any revolutionary sensibility to make his or her decision.

The New Society

Q: Once we reach a libertarian municipalist society, what if it turns out that civic virtue and direct-democratic institutions aren't enough to keep everyone in the community from acting in their own self-interest? All it might take is a few people trying to aggrandize themselves to spoil the whole communistic nature of the society. Would some kind of strictures have to be instituted that would enforce norms for the society? Would there be any laws in a libertarian municipalist society? Or a constitution?

A: Before I answer you specifically about the libertarian municipalist society, some historical background would be useful. In prehistory, for an unknown period of time, human society was structured around family groups—tribes and clans—in which blood relationships determined the rights and duties of individuals to each other. Anyone outside a tribe was regarded as a stranger or, to use Marx's very appropriate term, as inorganic—and hence was subject to arbitrary treatment by the tribe.

This had many implications for how people conceived of justice. Let us say someone committed a crime—a man from one tribe murdered a man from another tribe. The only way the crime could be expiated and the murderer punished would be if the relatives of the victim decided to take blood vengeance. Of course after a while the amount of bloodshed necessary to make reparation for an abuse was diminished, or a different kind of penalty besides blood was imposed, such as an obligation to hand over a certain number of cattle. The schedule of reparations was worked out at times very elaborately. But the system of justice still depended on vengeance—on the victim or the family taking revenge on the perpetrator.

It has been one of humanity's greatest advances, over the course of history, to have moved out of this biologically based system of justice, by which I mean one based on kinship or blood ties and vengeance, into a more rational—but not necessarily completely rational—system of justice. The *Eumenides* by Aeschylus depicts the Athenians in exactly that situation—where blood vengeance is replaced by reasoned justice: Orestes, who killed his mother, is finally judged not as one who killed a blood relation per se but by a jury on rational, discursive grounds. And he is acquitted, on the basis of universal standards of justice based on reason, not punished on the basis of blood vengeance. At this point reason is beginning to supplant custom, and society is beginning to supplant biology.

Of course, every biologically conditioned institution is a social institution as well. Human beings are not mere animals anymore. Yet it's very hard to separate the social from the biological at so early a level. But over the course of history there are degrees in which biology has given way to rationality and sociality. The rise of *nomos*, as the Greeks called it, or law—a rationally derived standard for justice, defining rights and duties—marks one of humanity's greatest ascents out of animality. It's not a culminating advance, but it is a basic advance.

I'm certainly not arguing that all laws are rational because they are laws; rather, I am claiming that the concept of *nomos* itself is rational. Law as a substitute for blood vengeance is a rational advance, even though many specific laws are very irrational. Ancient constitutions like Hammurabi's legal code accepted slavery, the domination of women by men—a large number of abusive features that would be untenable today and certainly inconceivable in a rational society. But Hammurabi's code did mark an advance out of blind custom, opening a realm of discussion about right and wrong behaviour. And in the case of the Athenian democracy, even more custom was shed and replaced by a reasoned consideration of rights and duties, evils and goods, harmful actions and beneficial actions.

A rational society by definition could do no less. In a libertarian municipalist society it would be necessary to fully explicate, on a rational basis, the rights and duties of people, the laws or *nomoi* of the society, and their modes of self-management. And these *nomoi* would derive from a rational constitution that the people who lived under it would draw up. That is to say, society would be constituted rationally, in the sense that the people would literally create a basic framework for it, guided by all the ethical considerations that reason and experience afford.

So yes, it would be necessary to have a constitution and to have *nomoi* that are as democratic, as rational, as flexible, and as creative as possible. To reject such a constitution and the *nomoi* that elaborate it would be to fall back once again on a system like blood vengeance. Or else we would fall back on arbitrary judgments, based on a mystical belief in an unshakable human nature that is magically benign. Such a view is completely absurd. It rests on the belief that people would always behave benignly toward others and toward their community, that they are inherently good, and that they have been "corrupted" by civilization. Any notion of a fixed human nature, even a benign one, as well as the myth of a "noble savage," is sociobiological nonsense. It renders people's behaviour completely inflexible and denies them one of their most important features, namely creativity, a signal feature of humans, as opposed to the adaptivity typical of animals.

So in a libertarian municipalist society, which I identify with a rational society and with libertarian communism, it would be vital to have a reasoned constitution with reasoned *nomoi*, one that would prevent authoritarianism and all the other undesirable features in the present society, like private property and the State. It would at the same time offer a positive form of law, providing reasoned ethical guidelines that are sufficiently flexible to allow for changing situations.

Q: How would these ideas specifically be applied in the development of a libertarian municipalist movement?

A: I would like to suggest that such a movement itself would have a constitution. In this respect I go against the libertarian opinion that wants a minimum of structure. As I've already said, where you have a minimum amount of structure, you have a maximum amount of arbitrariness. Serious and committed people always want organization; the question is, what kind? The dizzying dissoluteness one encounters among lifestyle anarchists today invariably ends up in mere smoke or in authoritarian manipulation, such as I saw in the antinuclear Clamshell alliance during the 1970s.

So the movement would have a constitution, with a preamble to state its larger goals and its character. And then it would specify as clearly as possible, albeit not frozen into inflexibility, how it is to function and, where an explanation is needed, why it is to function that way. The constitution would specify decision-making by majority rule voting, which in my view is indispensable. It would clearly specify how delegates are to be elected and recalled if necessary, and it would distinguish their powers from those of parliamentary-type representatives. It could include an account of municipal democracy and confederation.

Once a libertarian municipalist movement is established on the basis of a rational constitution, guided by rational *nomoi*, how would it go about calling for citizens' assemblies? Here in Burlington, during the late 1970s and early 1980s, the anarchist groups that I worked with were advocating citizens' assemblies in each of the city's six wards. We continued to call for them after a third-party Progressive was elected mayor of the city in 1981. This mayor, Bernard Sanders, seemed not to know what we were talking about, but he was prepared to go along with the idea because it sounded good. So his Progressive administration agreed to create a Neighbourhood Planning Assembly (NPA) in each ward. They weren't authentic citizens' assemblies—they were "planning assemblies," whose purpose was to be responsible for disbursing funds for community development. In terms of policy-making their role was strictly advisory. But at least in Vermont, the power of citizens in an assembly to mandate morally is often very compelling, and for a time—until many of our local anarchists began to fade into private life—they exercised considerable influence.

Q: In Vermont the system of local government and the political system that goes with it is a lot looser and more open than it is in other parts of the United States, not to speak of the world. Here ballot access is relatively easy and election laws are quite relaxed, so it might be easier to get a libertarian municipalist movement going here than in other places. In California, for example, it's much harder for new political groupings to get on the ballot. In France or even Canada the towns and cities are far more creatures of the State than they are here, and they're far more under the State's direct control. Certainly in most places it would be illegal for a citizens' assembly to legislate, as it were, to make policy for the locality. What can a libertarian municipalist movement do under such circumstances?

A: Yes, the establishment of NPAs in Burlington was the result of a concurrence of grassroots movements with a fairly sympathetic civic administration. I can foresee situations in which such a concurrence as we had here would not occur—indeed, where a city hall would stridently oppose the formation of quasi-legal citizens' assemblies, let alone ones with legal powers that would override those of the city council. Or where the city charter or town charter cannot yet be changed to give greater power to citizens' assemblies. In such cases it makes complete sense for the movement first to establish citizens' assemblies that have only moral authority—and in fact that was all the power the Burlington assemblies had anyway.

A libertarian municipalist movement would initiate citizens' assemblies, without necessarily gaining the consent of a city council but hopefully with sufficient support from the citizens in the specific neighborhood or ward or town. Or if assemblies already exist, the movement could to call for their recognition as legal bodies empowered to pass ordinances and laws—in other words *nomoi*. At the same time, needless to say, the movement would run candidates who would consistently demand the formation of these assemblies and/or their empowerment.

In the past, it was not unusual, in periods when institutions were fairly authoritarian, for moral institutions to begin to emerge. In medieval times many towns, without having any legal authority to do so, formed assemblies and created institutions that opposed those of the feudal lords or bishops who literally owned the city. The *ateneo* movement, which grew up in Spain under Franco, may be another example—it may well have played a role in diminishing the power of the Francoist State toward the end of Franco's life.

In any case, once a libertarian municipalist movement initiates extralegal assemblies, it's crucial that they be institutionalized, even if only on paper. What the movement should not do is call assemblies on an ad hoc basis, merely to discuss a specific issue, then drift away when the issue fades from public interest.

What I'm saying is that if a libertarian municipalist movement is going to initiate assemblies, it's not enough for it simply to call a meeting of the people, like a "town meeting," as they wrongly call them in New York City, to discuss or publicize a specific issue, and then let the existence of such assemblies drift away.

Rather, the assembly must be institutionalized—this is crucial—and it must have a distinct structure. It must meet regularly, whether it be once a month or once every few weeks or once a quarter. It must have a constitution, one that establishes residency requirements and all the necessary regulations that give it definition. It must have a name. It must have a moderator or facilitator, and at the very least, it must have a coordinating committee. It must have a system of communications—if possible, it should publish a periodical. During the course of its meetings it should have an agenda, one carefully prepared with the participation of community members. If there are a sufficient number of people, the assembly could elect various commissions to study issues and make recommendations.

If it's not clearly institutionalized, the assembly will become, to use the term ironically, a "floating signifier"—merely an obfuscatory semblance of what it might be. Lacking definition and institutionalization, it would merely be a forum and would not be taken seriously. Nor, in my opinion, would it conform with a libertarian municipalist social and political agenda. Libertarian municipalism seeks to exacerbate the tension between municipalities and the State, to become an oppositional dual power that will, under propitious conditions, abolish the State for a confederal system of social administration.

The assembly may very well turn into a genuine expression of opinion so emphatic that it reflects the community and recreates its political culture, or at least significantly modifies it. Assemblies may multiply, ultimately obliging city councils to recognize them and give them legal power.

All of this is a process, a development, one that will require a long struggle. Libertarian municipalism is not merely a strategy or a body of tactics, even though I've been obliged to use these terms in a limited way because we have yet to invent a language that expresses the features of a rational society. Nor is it a society that can be brought into existence by turning on a light switch. It's a rich idea, one that flows out of history itself. And fulfilling it will require dedication. It requires commitment, idealism, and rationality.

I can say this much: I completely agree with Marx that

capitalism is a system that must necessarily tear down this society by virtue of its guiding principle of production for the sake of production, growth for the sake of growth. Libertarian municipalism must not be compromised with reformist or lesser-evil notions, like creating another third party or engaging in "independent politics" within the framework of the Nation-State. Every compromise, especially a politics based on lesser evils, invariably leads to the greatest evils. It was through a series of lesser evils, the ones presented to Germans during the Weimar Republic, that Hitler came to power. Hindenburg, the last and least of all the evils, who was elected president in 1932, proceeded to appoint Hitler chancellor in 1933, bringing fascism to Germany, while the Social Democrats kept voting for one lesser evil after another until they got the worst of evils.

One has only to look at Statecraft today for more examples. In the United States, a President Bush or Dole would have had far more difficulty in dismantling the welfare system than did the "lesser evil" Bill Clinton. All the potential opposition that might have risen up to block that vicious act, even to protest against it, was politically blotted up by Clinton, whom liberals had long considered the "lesser evil" to a Republican president. So "lesser-evil-ism" has clearly become a formula for capitulation.

I don't know if such a social structure as I've tried to describe will come into being. It might not. I'm writing an essay on ethics now, and the opening line is: "Humanity is too intelligent not to live in a rational society. It remains to be seen whether it is intelligent enough to achieve one." I can only count on the emergence, sooner or later, of enough people who have the character, the insight, and the idealism, as people have long had on the left, to carry through this approach. But if such a movement does not emerge, one thing can be said with absolute certainty: Capitalism is not simply going to produce economic injustices. Given its law of accumulation, its grow-or-die imperative that stems from competition in the marketplac itself, it will definitely tear down social life. There can be no compromise with this social order.

Notes

1. Mogens Herman Hansen, *The Athenian Democracy in the Age of Demosthenes: Structure, Principles and Ideology*, trans. J. A. Crook (Oxford: Blackwell, 1991).

2. Gaston Leval, *Collectives in the Spanish Revolution*, trans. Vernon Richards (London: Freedom Press, 1975).

Appendix

❧

Electoral Platform of the Burlington Greens

The Burlington (Vermont) Greens used this document as their electoral platform in March 1989, when they ran two candidates for city council (which was then called the board of aldermen) and one for mayor, in a libertarian municipalist campaign. In addition, they issued a series of position papers and the first comprehensive report on Burlington's environment. The platform may serve here as an example of a transitional program.

Who Are the Burlington Greens?

We are working to create a new politics for Burlington—a politics that is based on ecology, the control of growth, a moral economy social justice, and a truly grassroots democracy.

We are working to create a new movement in Burlington—a movement that is not just another party for electing politicians to office, but one that involves ordinary people on an everyday basis in the political process in community and neighborhood organizations. We hope to develop a truly popular movement to address the causes of our social and ecological problems, not merely to deal with their symptoms on a patchwork basis.

I. Ecology and Growth
The Problem: The ecological crisis is the greatest single problem that faces our time. As the popular media have pointed out, the Earth itself is now endangered. The planet is literally dying. The ecological crisis raises searing problems that can no longer be ignored; nor is offering lip-service enough. There are highly specific local aspects of the ecological crisis that must be addressed through committed action at the local level. Of these, "growth" is now the most pressing.

Burlington is growing uncontrollably, with no regard for people's needs and with no respect for a balance between ourselves and our natural environment. We are faced with increased pollution, unsightly building projects, traffic congestion, and the destruction of our wetlands and the unique ecology of Lake Champlain. We are faced with the prospect of more and larger highways, the complete loss of open land in our city, and growing waste disposal problems. Chittenden County's cancer mortality rate is higher than that of Vermont as a whole. Big-city stresses are invading every aspect of our lives.

The Alternative: The Burlington Greens call for a moratorium on growth. It is essential that citizens be given the time to discuss the problems facing Burlington in open assemblies and to democratically decide how our community can develop along ecological, humanistic, and rational lines.

We call for the election of an Environmental Commission and the formation of a Citizens' Environmental Advisory Board, composed of representatives of environmental organizations, specialists who have no business or industrial ties, concerned citizens, city planners, and architects. This board would assist the Environmental Commission in developing ecological guidelines for future growth in Burlington and would provide citizens with an annual report on the status of our environment in our city and its surroundings.

We call for serious efforts to develop alternative energy sources like solar, wind, and methane power. The recycling and reduction of wastes should be a priority, as should the creation of a regional plan to share our local energy resources in a cooperative and democratic manner with neighboring communities.

We believe that the future of Burlington should be guided by ecological and human needs, not by special interests and "developers" who are profiting at the expense of the community.

II. A Moral Economy
The Problem: We live in a competitive grow-or-die economy that knows no moral or ecological limits. The market economy by its very nature must expand and expand until it tears down the planet. This insane form of growth is not only destroying the natural environment, it is also destroying the human community.

Although our local economy is "growing" at an unparalleled rate, it is not providing for such basic needs as decent housing and a livable income for many citizens. A growing class of underprivileged people is confronted with special problems that are worsening steadily. The self-seeking, competitive relationships spawned by the market economy are replacing cooperative, moral relationships between people.

The Alternative: We need to bring not only an ecological but a social ecological perspective to bear on the problems confronting our city. We should not pit ecological issues against social issues, trading off the natural environment for the dubious benefits of growth.

The Burlington Greens believe that decent housing, a livable income, and good working conditions are rights, not privileges. In the same way, we also believe that people have a natural right to live in a healthy, sound environment. We believe that practical steps can be initiated by our community to give some reality to these rights. We call for:

These are only stepping stones to what we hope will be a municipally controlled economy managed by the citizenry in free assemblies and guided by moral as well as ecological concerns.

III. Grassroots Democracy
The Problem: The ecological and social problems that face Burlington and the greater Burlington area are not being taken seriously because the people are being deprived of what little power they have as a result of a highly centralized city hall and governmental bureaucracy. Under the guise of "popular" leadership, a new breed of technocratic managers has reduced us from active citizens to passive taxpayers. Our Vermont heritage of participatory democracy is being subverted by technicians who are contemptuous of popular rule.

The Alternative: We need a new politics in our city, not just another administration. We call for authentic neighborhood assemblies with ever-expanding decision-making powers to establish social and ecological policy and to help administer our city. We believe that all major city commissions should be elected by the people, their terms limited to one year, and their number increased to countervail the centralization of power in the mayor's office and city hall. We call for charter revisions that will foster public self-governance in the Vermont tradition.

Considerable time should be set aside at aldermanic meetings for open discussion by citizens on a variety of issues, and child care should be provided free of charge for all parents wishing to participate. Citizens should also have the right to recall alderpeople who fail to live up to their mandates and their commitments to the city's wards.

We believe that Burlington should vigorously and unrelentingly lead the way to achieve home rule in Vermont so that towns and cities can govern their affairs as freely as possible without interference from the state. Burlington should also lead the way to establish democratic countywide confederations with neighboring communities to deal with regional concerns such as transportation, growth, and other economic and environmental problems.

IV. Social Justice
The Problem: We are witnessing the emergence of a new underclass of poor people, particularly women, who are suffering appalling poverty in the midst of incredible affluence. Sizable groups of people work at low-paying jobs. The elderly are neglected and warehoused, as are the homeless and those who cannot acquire decent housing. Gay and les-

bian people are discriminated against and often attacked because of their sexual orientation. Social injustice has become a major factor in the everyday life of our community.

The Alternative: We believe that Burlington should become "the most livable city" for all of its citizens. We call for the greening of Burlington! Green for us means ecology—and ecology means a harmonious, participatory community between human beings and other forms of life. But this in turn means that we must live in a harmonious, participatory human community. Without a community guided by ecological principles and social justice, we will see the deterioration of our environment on an appalling scale and the further destruction of everything that makes the Burlington area a livable place for ourselves and our children.

We believe that the feminization of poverty must be ended with decisive cooperative action. Women must be given decent and comparable pay for their work. Free child care should be provided for any parent who desires it. The problems of the homeless must be addressed by the community creatively, with an eye toward giving the homeless control

- a community–controlled municipal bank that will provide financial resources and low–interest loans for the purchase and repair of homes and for the initiation of innovative ecological housing projects for low–income groups

- bond issues and changes in local tax structures to provide for as much housing for the need and elderly as is necessary

- a direct network between farmers and consumers to foster local agriculture

- municipal acquisition of open land to be held in public trust for recreation, gardening, and parks

- municipally controlled cooperatives to develop and implement alternative technologies and to produce quality goods in accord with Vermont's reputation for craftsmanship.

over their housing. Services for the elderly must be expanded. Gentrification must be ended. Older neighborhoods must be upgraded structurally in the interests of the citizens who live in them today—not in the interest of privileged people who hope to invade them tomorrow.

The Burlington Greens do not think that these basic ecological and human goals—and many others that we hope to present to the public in position papers—are unrealistic or impossible to achieve. Some can be realized immediately; others will doubtless take some time. But we think they are minimum goals toward which all socially concerned, democratically oriented citizens should work. We think these goals can be achieved only through a movement that is antiauthoritarian and popular, one that seeks to create a grassroots democracy. We seek to change our entire image of progress as mindless growth into an ecological vision of progress that will ultimately foster a new harmony between people and between humanity and nature.

Help us create a new politics and a new movement!

For Further Reading

❧

Works on Libertarian Municipalism by Murray Bookchin

"Libertarian Municipalism: An Overview," *Green Perspectives*, no. 24 (Oct. 1991).*

"The Meaning of Confederalism," *Green Perspectives*, no. 20 (Nov. 1990). Republished in *Our Generation*, no. 22 (Fall 1990–Spring 1991), and in *Society and Nature*, vol. 1, no. 3 (1993), pp. 41–54.

"Radical Politics in an Era of Advanced Capitalism," *Green Perspectives*, no. 18 (Nov. 1989). Republished in *Our Generation*, vol. 21, no. 2 (Summer 1990).

Remaking Society: Pathways to a Green Future. Montreal: Black Rose Books; Boston: South End Press, 1989.

"The Greening of Politics," *Green Perspectives*, no. 1 (Jan. 1986).

From Urbanization to Cities, London: Cassell, 1995. Originally published as *The Rise of Urbanization and the Decline of Citizenship*, San Francisco: Sierra Club Books, 1987; subsequently republished in Canada as *Urbanization Without Cities*, Montreal: Black Rose Books, 1992.

"Theses on Libertarian Municipalism," *Our Generation*, vol. 16,

---

*To obtain back issues of *Green Perspectives*, please write to: The Social Ecology Project, P.O. Box 111, Burlington, Vermont 05402 U.S.A.

nos. 3–4 (Spring/Summer 1985). Republished in *The Limits of the City*, Montreal: Black Rose Books, 1986.

The Limits of the City. New York: Harper and Row Colophon Books, 1974; Montreal: Black Rose Books, 1986.

"Spring Offensives and Summer Vacations," *Anarchos*, no. 4 (1972).

Ancient Greek Democracy

Finley, M. I. *Democracy Ancient and Modern*. New Brunswick, NJ: Rutgers University Press, 1972.

Finley, M.I. *Politics in the Ancient World*. Cambridge and New York: Cambridge University Press, 1983.
Forrest, W. G. *The Emergence of Greek Democracy*. New York: McGraw Hill, 1966

Jaeger, Werner. *Paideia; The Ideals of Greek Culture*. New York: Oxford University Press, 1939.

Kitto, H.D.F. *The Greeks*. London: Penguin Books, 1951.

Zimmern, Alfred. *The Greek Commonwealth*. New York: Modern Library Editions, n.d.

Late Medieval and Early Modern Europe

Barber, Benjamin. *The Death of Communal Liberty: A History of Freedom in a Swiss Mountain Canton*. Princeton University Press, 1974.

Blockmans, Wim P. "Alternatives to Monarchical Centralisation: The Great Tradition of Revolt in Flanders and Brabant." In H.G.

Koenigsberger, ed., *Republicanism in Early Modern Europe.* Munich: Oldenbourg, 1988.

Castells, Manuel. *The City and the Grassroots: A Cross–Cultural Theory of Urban Social Movements.* Berkeley and Los Angeles: University of California Press, 1983. Chapter 2 gives an account of the *comunero* movement.

Laslett, Peter. *The World We Have Lost.* London: Methuen, 1965.

Martines, Lauro. *Power and Imagination: City–States in Renaissance Italy.* New York: Alfred A. Knopf, 1979.

Mundy, John H., and Peter Riesenberg. *The Medieval Town.* New York: Van Nostrand Reinhold, 1958.

Charles Tilly and Wim P. Blockmans, ed. *Cities and the Rise of States in Europe, A.D. 1000 to 1800.* Boulder, Colo.: Westview Press, 1994.

Waley, Daniel. *The Italian City–Republics.* New York: McGraw Hill, 1969.

New England Town Meeting

Breen, T.H. *Puritans and Adventurers: Change and Persistence in Early America.* New York: Oxford University Press, 1980.

Gross, Robert A. *The Minutemen and Their World.* New York: Hill and Wang, 1976.

Katz, Stanley N., ed. "Colonial Politics and Society: The Eighteenth Century," part 3 of *Colonial America: Essays in Political and Social Development.* Boston: Little, Brown, 1971.

Lingeman, Richard. *Small Town America: A Narrative History, 1620–Present.* New York: Putnam, 1980, chapter 1.

Lockridge, Kenneth A. *A New England Town: The First Hundred Years.* New York: W.W. Norton, 1970.

Morgan, Edmund S. *The Puritan Dilemma: The Story of John Winthrop.* Boston: Little, Brown, 1958.

Zuckerman, Michael. *Peaceable Kingdoms: New England Towns in the Eighteenth Century.* New York: Vintage, 1970.

The Parisian Sectional Assemblies in the French Revolution

Bookchin, Murray. *The Third Revolution.* London: Cassell, 1996.

Soboul, Albert. *The Sans–Culottes: The Popular Movement and Revolutionary Government, 1793–1794.* Vol.1. Trans. Remy Inglis Hall. Garden City, NY: Anchor/Doubleday, 1972.

Thompson, J. M. *The French Revolution.* Oxford: Basil Blackwell, 1943, esp. pp. 280–82, 295–98.

Cities and Confederations in the Twentieth Century

Bookchin, Murray. *The Spanish Anarchists.* New York: Harper and Row, 1977.

Castells, Manuel. " The Making of an Urban Social Movement: The Citizen Movement in Madrid towards the End of the Franquist Era," part 5 of *The City and the Grassroots: A Cross–Cultural Theory of Urban Social Movements.* Berkeley: University of California, 1983.

Gerecke, Kent, ed. *The Canadian City*. Montreal: Black Rose Books, 1991.

Gordon, David, ed. *Green Cities: Ecologically Sound Approaches to Urban Space*. Montreal: Black Rose Books, 1990.

Kotler, Milton. *Neighborhood Government*. New York: Bobbs–Merrill, 1969.

Roussopoulos, Dimitrios, ed. *The City and Radical Social Change*. Montreal: Black Rose Books, 1982.

Schecter, Stephen. *The Politics of Urban Liberation*. Montreal: Black Rose Books, 1978.

Murray Bookchin is one of North America's most important writers on environmental issues and has been active in the ecology movement for more than thirty years.

Professor Emeritus at the School of Environmental Studies, Ramapo College and Director Emeritus of the Institute of Social Ecology, he has authored more than a dozen books on urbanism, ecology, technology and philosophy.

PHILOSOPHY OF SOCIAL ECOLOGY
2nd edition

Everything ancient and modern is grist for criticism and few authors have a better understanding of this than Murray Bookchin.

Decades ago when the concern over the ecology centred around problems of conventional environmentalism, when environmental issues were seen in practical and limited terms that could be resolved by legislative action, public education, and personal example, Murray Bookchin was already at work formulating his unique philosophy of social ecology. This philosophy, that would serve in the highest ethical sense as a guide for human conduct and would provide an awareness of humanity's place in nature, is offered here in this second, revised edition of *The Philosophy of Social Ecology*.

This edition has been so radically revised that in many respects it is a new book. The essays that appeared in the first edition have remained, in their essentials, but many of Bookchin's original formulations have been significantly altered. There ia as well, a new Introduction, a new Preface and a new essay entitles "History, Civilization, and Progress"-written in 1994-which critically examines the social and ethical relativism so much in vogue today.

A useful corrective to simplistic thinking about the human predicament.
Canadian Book Review Annual

Bookchin expands upon the concept of natural evolution and delivers it from the trap of mechanistic thinking.
Imprint

Bookchin addresses a different body of concerns: the need by the public for an ecologically creative sensibility toward the environment.
La Géopraphie Appliquée

Bookchin penetrates, challenges, and radically changes some of the most fundamental assumptions in the ecology debate.
From My Bookshelf

183 pages
Paperback	**ISBN: 1-551640-18-X**	**$19.99**
Hardcover	**ISBN: 1-551640-19-8**	**$48.99**

DEFENDING THE EARTH*
Debate between Murray Bookchin & Dave Foreman
Introduction by David Levine
This book is the outcome the first public meeting between the 'social ecologists' and the deep 'ecologists'.

...contains eloquent passages by Bookchin, who has a clear and humane sense of human's obligation to fellow human and the natural world...worth reading.
Vermont Times

Defending the Earth is a must-read for anyone concerned with environmental or social justice.
Imprint

120 pages, index
Paperback ISBN: 0-921689-88-8 $15.99
Hardcover ISBN: 0-921689-73-X $48.99
L.C. No. 90-83628

THE ECOLOGY OF FREEDOM
The Emergence and Dissolution of Hierarchy; revised edition
The most systematic articulation of his ideas.
San Francisco Review of Books

A confirmation of his (Bookchin's) status as a penetrating critic not only of the ways in which humankind is destroying itself, but of the ethical imperative to live better.
Village Voice

Elegantly written, and recommended for a wide audience.
Library Journal

395 pages, index
Paperback ISBN: 0-921689-72-1 $19.99
Hardcover ISBN: 0-921689-73-X $48.99
L.C. No. 90-83628

LIMITS OF THE CITY
2nd revised edition

"City air makes people free." With this medieval adage, Bookchin begins a remarkable book on the evolution and dialectics of urbanism, wherein he argues, convincingly, that there was once a human and progressive tradition of urban life.

An antidote to superficial thinking.
Toronto Star

Valuable for its historical perspective and its discussion of the effects on the individual of the modern city.
The Humanist in Canada

194 pages, index
Paperback ISBN: 0-920057-64-0 $17.99
Hardcover ISBN:0-920057-34-9 $46.99

THE MODERN CRISIS*
2nd revised edition

A challenging treatise on social ecology, identifying it as society's only alternative to disaster.

Bookchin is invigorated by the inadequacies of the old isms...He sketches here a new ism called..."ecological ethics"...which is not based on self interest.
Kingston Whig-Standard

A worthwhile read. Bookchin is the prophet of the green revolution.
Libertarian Labor Review

194 pages
Paperback ISBN:0-920057-62-4 $18.99
Hardcover ISBN:0-920057-61-6 $47.99

POST-SCARCITY ANARCHISM
with a new introduction
8th printing

A new introduction by the author brings this classic up to the minute Bookchin's views, as recorded in this collection, continue to be sought out and debated by those committed to progressive thought and action. Breaks new ground in its discussion of freedom.*Bookchin's caustic comments are ever important, rarely finding an equal in the field of contemporary analysis.*

Canadian Book Review Annual
265 pages
Paperback ISBN:0-920057-39-X $19.99
Hardcover ISBN:0-920057-41-1 $48.99

REMAKING SOCIETY*

To anyone new to his work, here is a clear synthesis of Bookchin's ideas.

...an intellectual tour de force...the first synthesis of the spirit, logics, and goals of the European "Green Movement" available in English
Choice
208pages
Paperback ISBN:0-921689-02-0 $18.99
Hardcover ISBN:0-921689-03-9 $47.99

TOWARD AN ECOLOGICAL SOCIETY
3rd printing

Bookchin's great virtue is that he constantly relates his theories to society as it is.
George Woodcock

Bookchin is capable of penetrating, finely indignant historical analysis. Another stimulating collection.
In These Times

A work that gives abundant evidence of its author's position at the centre of the debate.
Telos
315 pages
Paperback ISBN:0-919618-98-7 $18.99
Hardcover ISBN:0-919618-99-5 $37.99

URBANIZATION WITHOUT CITIES
The Rise and Decline of Citizenship
revised edition

Bookchin argues for an ecological ethics and citizenry that will restore the balance between city and country.

To reverse the city's dehumanization, social thinker Bookchin here advocates an agenda for participatory democracy...It is significant.

Publisher's Weekly

340 pages, index

Paperback ISBN:1-895431-00-X   **$19.99**

Hardcover ISBN: 1-895431-01-8   **$48.99**

L.C. No. 91-072980

FINDING OUR WAY
Rethinking Ecofeminist Politics
by Janet Biehl

Inundated by advocates of "cultural feminism," Goddess worship, deep ecology, and post-modernism, today's ecofeminst movement has lost much of its critical and constructive voice. In *Finding Our Way*, feminist theorist Janet Biehl lays the groundwork for a new left ecofeminist politics.

Finding Our Way is must reading for anyone wishing to explore the philosophical connections between feminism, ecology, and the left.

... provides a sorely needed perspective on the relationship between feminism and ecology, most significantly how both feminism and ecology suffer when reason and critical social analysis are abandoned in favor of nature mythology, goddess worship, and mysticsm.

New Politics

210 pages

Paperback ISBN:0-921689-78-0   **$19.99**

Hardcover ISBN:0-921689-79-9   **$38.99**

L.C. No. 90-83625

BLACK ROSE BOOKS

has also published the following books of related interest

Anarchism and Ecology, by Graham Purchase

Manufacturing Consent: Noam Chomsky and the Media, edited by Mark Achbar

Decentralizing Power: Paul Goodman's Social Criticism, edited by Taylor Stoehr

Nature and the Crisis of Modernity, by Raymond A. Rogers

The Ecology of the Automobile, by Peter Freund and George Martin

Political Ecology, Dimtrios Roussopoulos

Balance: Art and Nature, by John Grande

Civilization and its Discontented, by John Laffey

Finding Our Way: Rethinking Eco-Feminist Politics by Janet Biehl

Aboriginal People: Toward Self-Government, edited by Marie Léger

A Nation within a Nation, by Marie-Anik Gagné

Pierre-Joseph Proudhon: A biography, by George Woodcock

William Goodwin: A biographical study, by George Woodcock

The Modern State: An Anarchist Analysis, by Frank Harrison

The Anarchist Movement: Reflections on Culture, Nature and Power, by John Clark

1984 and After, edited by Marsha Hewitt and Dimitrios Roussopoulos

The Anarchist Papers, edited by Dimitrios Roussopoulos

The Anarchist Papers 2, edited by Dimitrios Roussopoulos

The Anarchist Papers 3, edited by Dimitrios Roussopoulos

THE COLLECTED WORKS OF PETER KROPOTKIN
Memoirs of a Revolutionist; The Great French Revolution; Mutual Aid; The Conquest of Bread; Russian Literature; In Russian and French Prisons; Words of a Rebel; Ethics; Fields, Factories and Workshops; Fugitive Writings; Evolution and the Environment send for a free catalogue of all our titles

BLACK ROSE BOOKS
P.O. Box 1258
Succ. Place du Parc
Montreal, Quebec
H3W 2R3
Canada

To order books in North America:
(phone) 1-800-565-9523 (fax) 1-800-221-9985
In Europe: (phone) 081-986-485 (fax) 081-533-5821
Our Web Site address: http://www.web.net/blackrosebooks

PRINTED AND BOUND
IN BOUCHERVILLE, QUÉBEC, CANADA
BY MARC VEILLEUX IMPRIMEUR INC.
IN SEPTEMBER, 1997